Artificial Intelligence for Prompt Engineering

Mastering AI Prompt Engineering

Felix Anderson

Table of Contents

Artificial Intelligence for Prompt Engineering: Mastering AI Prompt Engineering

SECTION 5: Ethical & Practical Considerations in Prompt Engineering

Chapter 14: Bias, Ethics, and Responsible AI Prompting

- Recognizing Bias in AI Responses
- Ensuring Ethical and Inclusive AI Outputs
- Strategies for Reducing AI Bias Through Prompting
- **Illustration:** How AI Bias is Formed and Mitigated

Chapter 15: The Future of AI Prompt Engineering

- The Evolution of AI Models and Self-Improving Prompts
- Next-Generation AI Assistants and Personalized AI Agents
- AI-Generated Creativity and Its Implications
- The Role of Human Oversight in AI-Led Decision Making

Bonus Section: Additional Resources

- **Hands-On Exercises:** Real-World Prompting Challenges
- **Case Studies:** How Professionals Use AI Prompting in Different Industries
- **Prompt Library:** Ready-to-Use AI Prompts for Various Applications

Chapter 1

Introduction to AI Prompt Engineering

Defining Prompt Engineering

Artificial Intelligence (AI) has made **significant advancements** in natural language processing (NLP), enabling machines to understand and generate human-like text. However, the effectiveness of AI responses depends heavily on **how prompts are structured and framed**. This is where **prompt engineering** comes into play.

Prompt engineering is the **systematic process of designing and refining input instructions** given to an AI model to **elicit accurate, relevant, and high-quality responses**. It involves the use of carefully crafted phrases, structured queries, and guiding statements to ensure that AI interprets user intentions correctly.

At its core, **prompt engineering bridges the gap between human communication and machine understanding**. Without it, AI models often generate vague, off-topic, or incomplete responses. By crafting effective prompts, users can **harness the full power of AI**, maximizing its potential across various domains such as content generation, coding, research, and business applications.

Key Elements of Prompt Engineering

To define prompt engineering comprehensively, we need to break it down into its **key elements**:

1. **Clarity and Precision** – AI models process natural language based on statistical patterns. Vague or ambiguous prompts often result in **inaccurate** responses. **Example:**

   - **Vague Prompt:** "Tell me about Python."
   - **Clear Prompt:** "Explain the core features of Python programming, focusing on its role in machine learning."

2. **Contextual Framing** – AI lacks inherent knowledge of context unless it is **explicitly provided**. Effective prompts **establish clear context**, ensuring AI understands the scope and background of the query. **Example:**

   - **Without Context:** "Generate a summary."
   - **With Context:** "Summarize the key arguments in the article about climate change and renewable energy solutions."

3. **Instructional Guidance** – AI responds more effectively when given **explicit instructions** regarding **format, tone, or structure**. **Example:**

   - **Without Guidance:** "Describe a smartphone."
   - **With Guidance:** "Write a detailed product description of a smartphone, highlighting its camera features, battery life, and design."

4. **Length and Conciseness** – The prompt should be **detailed enough** to provide sufficient guidance while being **concise enough** to avoid unnecessary complexity.

5. **Iterative Refinement** – Prompt engineering is an **iterative process**. The effectiveness of a prompt can be **evaluated, refined, and improved** based on the AI's output.

Types of Prompts in AI

Prompt engineering utilizes **various prompting techniques** depending on the nature of the query and the desired response:

Prompt Type	Description	Example
Direct Prompting	A straightforward question or instruction.	"What is the capital of France?"
Role-Based Prompting	Assigning AI a role to tailor responses.	"You are an AI tutor. Explain Newton's Laws of Motion in simple terms."
Chain-of-Thought Prompting	Encouraging AI to **explain step-by-step reasoning**.	"Solve this math problem step by step: 345 × 12."

Few-Shot Prompting	Providing examples before the main query.	"Translate the following sentences into Spanish: 1. Hello, how are you? 2. I love programming."

Through **prompt engineering**, AI models can be **optimized** to generate **more relevant, logical, and useful responses**, making them valuable assets in multiple industries.

The Role of Prompt Engineering in AI Performance

Prompt engineering plays a **crucial role** in determining how effectively AI models **understand, process, and generate responses**. An AI model—no matter how advanced—**relies entirely on the input it receives**. A poorly structured prompt can result in **irrelevant, biased, or incomplete outputs**, whereas a well-engineered prompt ensures **accurate and useful results**.

How Prompt Engineering Impacts AI Performance

1. **Enhances Response Accuracy** – Well-structured prompts **reduce ambiguity**, ensuring AI **interprets user intent correctly**.
2. **Reduces Model Biases** – AI models learn from vast datasets, which may contain **inherent biases**. Properly designed prompts **mitigate bias** by directing the AI toward **neutral, balanced outputs**.
3. **Optimizes Efficiency** – AI models operate within a **token limit** (word count constraints). Efficient prompts **maximize output quality while minimizing wasted tokens**.
4. **Improves User Experience** – AI-driven applications, such as **chatbots and virtual assistants**, depend on well-engineered prompts for **seamless, human-like interactions**.
5. **Increases AI Adaptability** – Different AI models (e.g., GPT-4, Bard, Claude) **respond uniquely** to prompts. By refining prompts, users can **adapt AI behavior** to specific tasks.

Case Study: Prompt Engineering in Real-World Applications

Example 1: AI in Customer Support

- **Poor Prompt:** "Generate a response for a customer complaint."

- **Optimized Prompt:** "Write a professional email apologizing to a customer for a delayed shipment and offering a 10% discount as compensation."

Example 2: AI for Content Generation

- **Poor Prompt:** "Write a blog post about fitness."
- **Optimized Prompt:** "Write a 1000-word blog post about effective home workouts, including warm-up exercises, strength training, and cardio routines."

Through **proper prompt engineering**, AI becomes a **powerful tool** that **enhances productivity, creativity, and efficiency** across diverse sectors.

Evolution of AI Prompting and Language Models

The field of **AI prompt engineering** has evolved alongside **natural language processing (NLP)** and **machine learning models**. Early AI systems relied on **rigid command-based inputs**, but **modern AI models** can interpret **complex language queries** with remarkable accuracy.

Early AI and Rule-Based Systems

- Early **chatbots and virtual assistants** (e.g., ELIZA in 1966) used **predefined rules** to respond to user input.
- These models **lacked adaptability**, requiring **manual programming** for each response.

Rise of NLP and Machine Learning

- The emergence of **statistical NLP** enabled AI to learn from **large text datasets**.
- Early models like **word2vec (2013)** and **GloVe (2014)** helped AI understand **semantic relationships** between words.

The Deep Learning Revolution

- The introduction of **Transformer models (2017)** changed NLP forever.
- **BERT (2018)** introduced **contextual understanding**, improving AI's ability to process human language.

- **GPT-3 (2020)** showcased **massive-scale AI prompting**, leading to today's **AI-driven assistants**.

Modern AI and the Era of Prompt Engineering

- **GPT-4, Bard, Claude, and LLaMA** can process **long, complex prompts** with near-human reasoning.
- Prompt engineering techniques like **few-shot learning, chain-of-thought prompting, and role-based instructions** optimize AI performance.

Future of AI Prompting

- **AI models will become more autonomous**, reducing the need for manual prompt refinement.
- **Personalized AI assistants** will **adapt prompts dynamically** based on user preferences.
- **Multimodal AI models** will allow users to prompt AI using **text, images, and voice commands**.

AI Model	Year	Key Advancement
ELIZA	1966	Rule-based chatbot
word2vec	2013	Word embeddings for NLP
BERT	2018	Context-aware AI understanding
GPT-3	2020	Large-scale language model
GPT-4	2023	Advanced reasoning, multimodal AI

The rapid evolution of **AI and NLP** has made **prompt engineering a critical skill**, ensuring that AI-generated responses are **accurate, ethical, and effective**.

Why AI Models Need Effective Prompts

Artificial intelligence models, particularly those in natural language processing (NLP), **do not inherently understand human language** in the way humans do. Instead, they analyze vast amounts of data, recognize patterns, and generate responses based on probability. This makes **prompt engineering essential** for directing AI to produce meaningful, relevant, and contextually appropriate outputs.

The Importance of Effective Prompts

A **well-structured prompt** serves as the bridge between human intent and AI-generated output. Without precise instructions, AI models **may misinterpret queries, generate inaccurate information, or produce vague responses**. Here are several key reasons why AI models require **effective prompt engineering**:

1. Ensuring Accuracy and Relevance

AI models **generate responses based on statistical likelihoods**, meaning they prioritize responses that seem most probable rather than necessarily being factually correct. A **clear and well-defined prompt** ensures the AI focuses on the **right context** and minimizes errors.

- **Ineffective Prompt:** "Tell me about Python."
- **Effective Prompt:** "Explain the primary features of the Python programming language, including its data types, control structures, and object-oriented principles."

2. Reducing Ambiguity in AI Responses

AI models struggle with **ambiguity** unless **clear context** is provided. A vague prompt can lead to **generalized or incorrect answers**.

- **Without Context:** "Summarize the article."

- **With Context:** "Summarize the main arguments of the article on climate change, focusing on the impact of fossil fuels and renewable energy solutions."

3. Controlling the Format and Structure of AI Outputs

By specifying the format, users can **tailor AI responses** for different use cases such as **blog posts, emails, essays, or reports**.

- **Generic Request:** "Explain machine learning."
- **Formatted Request:** "Write a 500-word beginner-friendly guide explaining machine learning, including examples and practical applications."

4. Improving AI Performance in Multi-Step Tasks

Some tasks require **step-by-step reasoning** rather than a single response. **Prompt engineering** enables AI to **break down problems systematically**.

- **Simple Prompt:** "Solve 45 × 12."
- **Better Prompt:** "Solve 45 × 12 step by step, explaining each calculation in detail."

5. Preventing AI Hallucinations

AI models sometimes generate **false or misleading information**, commonly referred to as **hallucinations**. Effective prompting **guides AI to verify and fact-check responses**.

- **Uncontrolled:** "List the works of Albert Einstein." (AI may hallucinate non-existent works)
- **Refined:** "List the published works of Albert Einstein based on verifiable sources."

6. Enhancing User Experience in AI Applications

AI-powered **chatbots, virtual assistants, and automation tools** rely on **high-quality prompts** to deliver helpful, human-like interactions. Poorly structured prompts can lead to robotic, confusing, or irrelevant replies.

Example: AI Customer Service

- **Poor Prompt:** "Respond to a customer complaint."

- **Effective Prompt:** "Draft a professional email apologizing to a customer for a delayed shipment, offering a 10% discount as compensation, and assuring them of faster processing in the future."

Effective prompt engineering is essential for **maximizing the potential of AI models**, ensuring **accuracy, efficiency, and contextual awareness**.

Overview of AI Models: ChatGPT, Bard, Claude, LLaMA

Different AI models have been developed to **handle natural language processing** tasks, each with its **unique features, capabilities, and optimizations**. Let's explore some of the most prominent AI models used for **prompt engineering**.

1. ChatGPT (OpenAI)

Overview

ChatGPT is a **large language model (LLM)** developed by OpenAI, based on the **GPT (Generative Pre-trained Transformer) architecture**. It is designed to **generate human-like text, answer questions, and assist with various NLP tasks**.

Key Features

- **Conversational AI** – Designed to **simulate human-like dialogue**.
- **Context Retention** – Maintains a conversation **across multiple turns**.
- **Fine-Tuned Responses** – Can be guided using **structured prompts**.
- **Code Generation** – Assists with programming tasks in **Python, JavaScript, and other languages**.

Example Prompts for ChatGPT

Task	Example Prompt
Content Writing	"Write a 1000-word article about blockchain technology and its applications."
Coding Assistance	"Write a Python function to sort a list of dictionaries by a specific key."
Research & Analysis	"Summarize the key findings of the latest AI research paper on deep learning."

2. Bard (Google AI)

Overview

Bard, developed by Google AI, is a **conversational AI system powered by PaLM 2 (Pathways Language Model)**. It focuses on providing **real-time, up-to-date information** and is **integrated with Google Search**.

Key Features

- **Access to Real-Time Data** – Unlike some AI models, Bard can **fetch live information**.
- **Google Search Integration** – Can pull information from Google's **vast knowledge base**.
- **Natural Language Understanding** – Capable of **interpreting complex queries**.

Example Prompts for Bard

Task	Example Prompt

Fact-Based Query	"What are the latest advancements in renewable energy as of 2024?"
Comparative Analysis	"Compare the features of iPhone 15 and Samsung Galaxy S24."
Travel Assistance	"Suggest a 7-day itinerary for a trip to Japan, including cultural sites and food experiences."

3. Claude (Anthropic AI)

Overview

Claude, developed by **Anthropic AI**, is designed with **safety and alignment in mind**, focusing on ethical and controlled AI responses.

Key Features

- **AI Safety Measures** – Designed to **reduce biases and harmful outputs**.
- **Transparency and Explainability** – Offers **clear reasoning** for responses.
- **Ethical AI Usage** – Ensures **responsible AI-generated content**.

Example Prompts for Claude

Task	Example Prompt
Ethical AI Advice	"How can AI be used responsibly in social media moderation?"
Legal Writing	"Draft a privacy policy for a mobile app following GDPR regulations."

Educational Explanation	"Explain quantum mechanics in simple terms for a high school student."

4. LLaMA (Meta AI)

Overview

LLaMA (Large Language Model Meta AI) is Meta's **open-source language model**, designed to be **lightweight, efficient, and scalable**.

Key Features

- **Optimized for Research and Development** – Focuses on **AI experimentation and learning**.
- **Lower Computational Requirements** – More **accessible to developers and researchers**.
- **Open-Source Model** – Allows **customization and modifications**.

Example Prompts for LLaMA

Task	Example Prompt
AI Research	"What are the limitations of current transformer-based language models?"
Educational AI	"Describe the history and evolution of artificial intelligence in 500 words."
Programming Support	"Explain the concept of recursion with a Python example."

Diagram: Evolution of AI Prompt Engineering

The **evolution of AI prompting** can be visualized in the following diagram, showing the shift from **rule-based NLP systems** to **modern, context-aware AI models**:

plaintext
CopyEdit

```
    +----------------------+     +------------------------+
+----------------------+     +------------------------+
   |  Rule-Based NLP (1960s) | -> |  Statistical NLP (1990s)
| -> |  Transformer Models (2017) | -> |  Prompt Engineering
(2020s) |
    +----------------------+     +------------------------+
+----------------------+     +------------------------+

    1. Rule-Based: Simple chatbots (e.g., ELIZA, 1966)
    2. Statistical NLP: Machine learning-based text analysis
(word2vec, GloVe)
    3. Transformer Models: Context-aware AI (BERT, GPT-3)
    4. Prompt Engineering: Optimized AI-human interaction
(GPT-4, Bard, Claude, LLaMA)
```

This progression highlights how AI has **shifted from rigid, predefined responses to highly adaptable, conversational models**, making **prompt engineering a crucial skill** in today's AI landscape.

The Influence of Prompt Structure on AI Responses

AI models, particularly **large language models (LLMs)** such as GPT-4, Bard, Claude, and LLaMA, **do not think or reason like humans**. Instead, they **predict the most probable sequence of words** based on vast amounts of training data. The way a **prompt is structured** plays a crucial role in determining **how AI interprets and responds to queries**.

Why Prompt Structure Matters

The effectiveness of an AI-generated response depends on how the prompt is framed. **A well-structured prompt** ensures:

1. **Clarity** – AI understands exactly what is being asked.
2. **Context** – AI maintains focus on the subject.
3. **Specificity** – AI provides relevant and precise information.
4. **Format Guidance** – AI structures its response appropriately.
5. **Completeness** – AI includes all necessary details without unnecessary additions.

Conversely, **poorly structured prompts** often lead to **vague, irrelevant, or incomplete responses**. They can cause the AI to:

- Misinterpret the intent.
- Generate generic or inaccurate information.
- Provide responses that lack structure or coherence.

Chapter 2

How AI Interprets Prompt Structure

AI models use **pattern recognition and token prediction** to generate responses. A well-structured prompt **guides the model** to generate text that aligns with user expectations.

Key Components of an Effective Prompt

1. **Directive Clarity:**
   - Use **precise and direct** language.
   - Avoid **vague or ambiguous** wording.
2. **Contextual Framing:**
   - Provide background information for **better understanding**.
3. **Explicit Instructions:**
   - Specify the **format and length** of the expected response.
4. **Constraints and Parameters:**
   - Define **boundaries or limitations** for AI-generated content.

Prompt Structure Types

Prompt Type	Effect on AI Response	Example
Open-ende d Prompt	Generates **broad, general responses**.	"Tell me about artificial intelligence."
Guided Prompt	Produces **focused and structured** answers.	"Explain artificial intelligence, its applications, and limitations in 500 words."
Comparati ve Prompt	AI analyzes **two or more items**.	"Compare Python and JavaScript for web development."
Step-by-St ep Prompt	Encourages **logical reasoning**.	"Explain how neural networks work, step by step."

By structuring prompts effectively, users can **enhance AI accuracy**, **reduce randomness**, and **improve usability** in professional and academic settings.

Examples of Good vs. Poorly Structured Prompts

Now that we understand the influence of **prompt structure on AI performance**, let's analyze real-world examples of **good vs. poorly structured prompts**.

1. Content Writing Prompts

Poorly Structured Prompt	Effect	Improved Prompt	Effect
"Write about marketing."	Too **vague** and lacks **specific direction**.	"Write a 1000-word blog on digital marketing trends in 2024, including SEO, social media strategies, and content marketing best practices."	AI generates a **detailed and structured** article with relevant sections.

2. Technical Coding Prompts

Poorly Structured Prompt	Effect	Improved Prompt	Effect
"Write a Python script."	No **specific task provided**.	"Write a Python script to scrape product data from an e-commerce website using BeautifulSoup."	AI generates **relevant code** instead of generic output.

3. AI-Powered Customer Support

Poorly Structured Prompt	Effect	Improved Prompt	Effect
"Help a customer."	Too **vague**; AI lacks **context**.	"Write a polite email apologizing to a customer for late delivery, offering a 10% discount for their next order."	AI generates **customer-friendly, context-aware** responses.

4. Research-Based AI Queries

Poorly Structured Prompt	Effect	Improved Prompt	Effect
"Explain global warming."	AI response may be **generic and unfocused**.	"Explain the causes, effects, and potential solutions to global warming, with scientific evidence and case studies."	AI delivers a **well-researched, structured response**.

Takeaway: **The more specific, structured, and directive a prompt is, the better AI performs** in producing high-quality responses.

Illustration: How AI Breaks Down Prompts into Tokens

AI models **do not process language like humans**. Instead, they **break down text into small units called tokens** before predicting the next most likely sequence.

What Are Tokens?

- **Tokens can be words, subwords, or even single characters.**
- **Common words** (e.g., "the", "cat") may be **single tokens**.
- **Longer words** may be split into **multiple tokens**.
- **Sentences are tokenized before AI processes them**.

Example: Tokenization in AI Models

Consider the sentence:
 "Artificial Intelligence is transforming businesses worldwide."

Word	Tokenized Representation
"Artificial"	artificial
"Intelligence"	intelligence
"is"	is
"transforming"	trans + forming
"businesses"	business + es
"worldwide"	world + wide

Here, words like **"transforming"** and **"businesses"** are broken into **subword tokens** to optimize processing.

Why Tokenization Matters in Prompt Engineering

- AI models **do not "read" words directly**—they **process numerical token IDs**.
- The **length of a prompt affects response quality** due to **token limits** in AI models.
- Well-structured prompts **reduce unnecessary tokenization**, improving **accuracy and efficiency**.

Illustration: How AI Tokenizes Prompts

plaintext
CopyEdit

```
Prompt: "Explain blockchain technology in simple terms."
    ↓
Tokenized: ["Explain", "block", "chain", "technology", "in",
"simple", "terms", "."]
    ↓
AI Processes Tokens & Predicts Next Sequence:
    ↓
AI Response: "Blockchain is a decentralized technology used to
record transactions securely."
```

This visualization shows how AI **processes prompts as numerical sequences** rather than whole words, reinforcing the need for **concise, well-structured prompts**.

Key Takeaways

- **Prompt structure directly influences AI output.**
- **Poorly structured prompts** lead to **vague or inaccurate responses**, while **well-structured prompts** ensure clarity and relevance.
- AI models **tokenize text**, breaking words into numerical representations.
- **Effective prompt engineering minimizes token wastage**, leading to **more precise AI responses**.

By mastering **prompt engineering**, users can **significantly improve AI performance**, ensuring **reliable, high-quality responses** across various applications.

Chapter 3

Key Components of a Well-Designed Prompt

Importance of Clarity, Specificity, and Context

Artificial intelligence models rely on **pattern recognition, token-based processing, and probability-driven text generation** to understand and respond to prompts. However, unlike humans, AI lacks **intrinsic reasoning or common sense**—it only processes language based on statistical correlations. This makes the **clarity, specificity, and context** of a prompt essential in ensuring high-quality responses.

Why Clarity Matters

A **clear prompt** eliminates ambiguity and **helps AI generate precise and relevant responses**. Poorly structured prompts **increase the likelihood of vague, misleading, or incorrect outputs**.

- **Unclear Prompt:** "Write about finance."
- **Clear Prompt:** "Write a 1000-word article on the fundamentals of personal finance, covering budgeting, saving, and investment strategies."

In the **unclear prompt**, AI lacks direction and may generate **generalized or irrelevant content**. The **clear prompt** ensures AI **stays focused** on personal finance and provides an **organized response**.

Why Specificity is Crucial

AI models generate responses based on **probability and learned data patterns**. If a prompt is **too broad**, the AI may produce **generic, unfocused, or unhelpful answers**. **Specificity** helps **narrow the scope** of AI-generated content.

- **Vague Prompt:** "Explain space exploration."
- **Specific Prompt:** "Explain the impact of private companies like SpaceX and Blue Origin on space exploration, including advancements in reusable rockets."

The **specific prompt** ensures AI **focuses on a particular aspect of space exploration,** leading to a **more insightful and structured response.**

The Role of Context in AI Responses

Context is essential because AI **does not inherently remember previous interactions** unless explicitly provided. A **contextual prompt** gives AI the necessary background to **generate more accurate and meaningful outputs.**

Scenario	Prompt Without Context	Prompt With Context
Technical Explanati on	"Explain blockchain."	"Explain blockchain technology as it applies to supply chain management, focusing on transparency and efficiency improvements."
Historical Analysis	"Describe World War II."	"Describe the causes and outcomes of World War II, focusing on the role of the United States in the conflict."
Marketing Strategy	"How do businesses use social media?"	"How do businesses use Instagram and TikTok for marketing, specifically in the fashion industry?"

Without context, AI provides **generic responses.** By **embedding context within the prompt,** users ensure **AI delivers targeted, useful, and insightful answers.**

The Balance Between Precision and Flexibility

An effective prompt **strikes a balance** between **being precise enough** to get a high-quality response and **flexible enough** to allow AI to generate creative or broad-ranging outputs.

The Risk of Over-Precision

A **highly precise** prompt may **restrict AI too much**, leading to a **rigid, overly narrow response**. Overly restrictive prompts may result in **limited, robotic, or overly structured answers**.

- **Overly Precise Prompt:** "Write a 200-word summary on how the electric vehicle industry grew between 2010 and 2023, mentioning Tesla, Rivian, and BYD, but avoiding any mention of government subsidies or battery advancements."
- **Effect:** AI **struggles** to provide meaningful insights due to **excessive constraints**.

A better approach would be:

- **Optimized Prompt:** "Write a summary of the growth of the electric vehicle industry from 2010 to 2023, highlighting major players like Tesla, Rivian, and BYD, while focusing on key market trends."

This **adjusted prompt** keeps precision but **allows AI some flexibility** to produce **a more engaging and informative response**.

The Risk of Over-Flexibility

A **highly flexible** prompt **lacks necessary details**, which often results in **generic, off-topic, or inaccurate AI responses**.

- **Overly Flexible Prompt:** "Tell me about cars."

- **Effect:** AI may generate **a broad and unfocused response**, covering **various aspects (history, engineering, brands, and types)** without depth in any specific area.

- **Optimized Prompt:** "Provide an overview of electric vehicles, including their environmental impact, cost-effectiveness, and future growth trends."

This revised prompt **guides AI toward a specific area** without **over-restricting creativity or contextual expansion**.

Achieving the Right Balance

21

A **well-balanced prompt** provides **clear objectives and necessary details** while allowing **room for AI to generate a meaningful response**.

Poorly Structured Prompt	Effect	Optimized Prompt	Effect
"Describe technology."	Too broad; AI produces **unfocused content**.	"Describe recent advancements in artificial intelligence, including GPT-4 and its real-world applications."	AI **delivers a targeted response**.
"Write a short story."	Too open-ended; AI may **generate random themes**.	"Write a short science fiction story about a future where AI governs society, but a group of rebels challenges its rule."	AI **produces a coherent, structured narrative**.
"Give me business advice."	Too vague; AI **doesn't know what area to focus on**.	"Provide five marketing strategies for a startup looking to increase online engagement."	AI **offers structured and actionable insights**.

Balancing **precision and flexibility** ensures that AI produces **accurate, relevant, and context-aware responses**.

How Length and Syntax Affect AI Responses

The **length and structure** of a prompt directly influence **how AI interprets and responds**. While **concise prompts** help in quick responses, **overly short prompts can lead to generic outputs**. On the other hand, **overly long or complex prompts** may cause AI to **lose focus or generate truncated responses**.

Effect of Prompt Length on AI Output

Prompt Length	Example	Effect on AI Response
Too Short	"Explain Python."	AI provides a **generic, broad explanation** with no depth.
Moderate (Optimal)	"Explain Python programming, covering its use in AI, web development, and automation."	AI **generates a well-structured, relevant response**.
Too Long	"Explain Python programming in detail, including its syntax, data types, functions, object-oriented programming, web development frameworks, data science applications, and how it compares to Java and C++."	AI **may lose focus or generate an overly long response** that cuts off key points.

How Syntax Influences AI Responses

AI **processes structured language more effectively** than unstructured input. **Well-formed syntax** ensures clarity and precision.

- **Poor Syntax:** "Tell importance technology"
- **Refined Prompt:** "Explain the importance of technology in modern businesses and its impact on productivity."

Why this matters:

- Proper syntax **eliminates ambiguity**.
- AI **processes well-formed instructions faster**.
- Structured syntax **guides AI toward precise responses**.

Best Practices for Prompt Length and Syntax

1. **Avoid Overly Short Prompts** – Provide **enough details** for AI to generate meaningful responses.
2. **Use Natural Sentence Structure** – Avoid unnatural phrasing that confuses AI.

3. **Break Down Complex Queries** – If necessary, **split multi-part prompts** into sequential instructions.

Optimizing Prompt Length and Syntax

Poorly Structured Prompt	Optimized Prompt
"What is history?"	"Provide an overview of world history, highlighting major civilizations and key historical events."
"How to do business online?"	"Explain how to start an online business, covering business models, digital marketing, and e-commerce strategies."
"Tell about Mars."	"Describe Mars, focusing on its atmosphere, surface conditions, and recent NASA exploration missions."

By maintaining **well-structured, context-rich, and well-balanced prompts**, AI models generate **coherent, targeted, and relevant responses**. Mastering **prompt clarity, specificity, and structure** ensures **better engagement, accuracy, and usability in AI interactions**.

Examples of Effective and Ineffective Prompts

Prompt engineering is a **strategic approach** to optimizing AI-generated responses. The quality of a prompt **directly influences** the accuracy, relevance, and usefulness of AI outputs. Poorly constructed prompts **lead to vague, off-topic, or incomplete answers**, while well-structured prompts ensure **clarity, depth, and contextual accuracy**.

To illustrate the impact of **effective vs. ineffective prompts**, let's analyze real-world examples across different domains, including **content creation, technical support, coding, business, research, and creative writing**.

---

1. Content Writing Prompts

Scenario: Writing an article on artificial intelligence

Ineffective Prompt	Problem	Effective Prompt	Why It Works
"Write about AI."	Too vague; AI does not know what aspects to cover.	"Write a 1500-word article on artificial intelligence, explaining its history, key breakthroughs, ethical concerns, and future trends."	Provides clear **scope, word count, and key focus areas**.
"Tell me about AI."	No direction; AI might generate generic information.	"Explain AI's role in healthcare, focusing on medical diagnostics, robotic surgery, and drug discovery."	AI generates a **focused and detailed** response.

2. Technical Support Prompts

Scenario: Requesting AI assistance for troubleshooting a technical issue

Ineffective Prompt	Problem	Effective Prompt	Why It Works

| "Fix my internet." | Too broad; AI does not know what issue to address. | "Provide step-by-step troubleshooting for a home Wi-Fi connection that frequently disconnects." | AI generates **specific diagnostic steps**. |
| "My computer is slow." | No specific details; AI cannot provide targeted solutions. | "Suggest five troubleshooting steps to improve the performance of a Windows 11 PC with 8GB RAM and an SSD." | AI tailors **solutions based on OS and hardware**. |

3. Coding and Programming Prompts

Scenario: Using AI to generate or debug code

Ineffective Prompt	Problem	Effective Prompt	Why It Works
"Write a Python script."	Too generic; AI does not know the task.	"Write a Python script that scrapes product data from an e-commerce website using BeautifulSoup."	AI generates **specific and usable** code.
"Fix this error."	No error message provided; AI cannot debug without details.	"I am getting a 'TypeError: unsupported operand type(s)' in Python. Explain the possible causes and how to fix them."	AI **diagnoses the issue and suggests fixes**.

4. Business and Marketing Prompts

Scenario: AI-generated business strategies

26

Ineffective Prompt	Problem	Effective Prompt	Why It Works
"Help me with marketing."	Too broad; AI cannot determine the marketing need.	"Suggest five digital marketing strategies for a startup launching a new fitness app."	AI provides **industry-specific insights**.
"Write an email."	No details; AI does not know the purpose or audience.	"Write a professional email introducing our new subscription-based SaaS product to potential enterprise clients."	AI generates a **well-structured email with the right tone**.

5. Research and Data Analysis Prompts

Scenario: AI-assisted research queries

Ineffective Prompt	Problem	Effective Prompt	Why It Works
"Tell me about climate change."	Too general; AI may generate an overwhelming amount of broad information.	"Summarize the key causes of climate change, citing recent scientific studies published after 2020."	AI **focuses on recent, science-backed insights**.
"Give me a list of famous inventors."	No context on the field or time period.	"List five famous inventors in the field of renewable energy and their contributions."	AI generates **a targeted and useful response**.

6. Creative Writing Prompts

Scenario: AI-generated creative content

Ineffective Prompt	Problem	Effective Prompt	Why It Works
"Write a story."	No theme, genre, or length specified.	"Write a 1000-word science fiction story about a human colony on Mars facing an unknown alien threat."	AI produces **structured, thematic storytelling**.
"Make a poem."	No style, topic, or tone given.	"Write a Shakespearean-style sonnet about lost love and redemption."	AI generates **a poem that follows a structured poetic form**.

Table: Dos and Don'ts of Prompt Engineering

A well-structured prompt ensures **AI generates precise, relevant, and valuable responses**. The following table outlines **best practices (Dos) and common mistakes (Don'ts) in prompt engineering**.

Dos	Don'ts
Be **clear and specific** in what you want AI to generate.	Avoid vague, open-ended prompts without context.

Provide **necessary context** to ensure relevant answers.	Don't assume AI understands implicit references—AI needs explicit instructions.
Use **role-based prompting** to improve response accuracy (e.g., "You are an AI writing assistant. Generate a blog post on AI ethics.").	Avoid general instructions like "Write a blog post."
Define **format expectations** (e.g., "Summarize in bullet points" or "Write in a formal business tone.").	Don't assume AI knows the preferred response format.
Test and **refine prompts iteratively** to improve AI outputs.	Don't rely on a single attempt—adjust prompts based on response quality.
Use **examples or few-shot prompting** when needed (e.g., "Translate these sentences: 1. Hello, how are you? → 2. Nice to meet you. →").	Avoid leaving AI to infer patterns when a few-shot example could clarify expectations.
Include **constraints** if needed (e.g., "Explain neural networks in simple terms for a high school student.").	Don't expect AI to self-adjust complexity levels without guidance.
Use **chain-of-thought prompting** for reasoning-based tasks (e.g., "Explain step by	Avoid under-specifying logical steps—AI may skip details.

step how an AI chatbot processes user queries.").	
Keep prompts **concise yet informative** to maximize response quality.	Don't make prompts overly long or complex, which may confuse AI.
Set **word limits or structured output formats** if needed (e.g., "Provide a 200-word summary of blockchain technology.").	Don't assume AI will provide concise responses without explicit instruction.

Key Takeaways

- **Effective prompts** guide AI **toward accurate, relevant, and structured responses**.
- **Ineffective prompts** lead to **generic, off-topic, or incorrect AI outputs**.
- Using **context, structure, and precision** improves **AI usability across various tasks**.
- **Prompt refinement** is essential—adjusting prompts **iteratively** leads to **better responses**.

By applying **prompt engineering best practices**, users can **harness the full potential of AI** to generate **high-quality, domain-specific content** tailored to their needs.

Chapter 4

Basic Prompting Methods

Direct vs. Contextual Prompts

Introduction to Prompting Approaches

Effective AI interactions depend on how prompts are structured. Two primary types of prompts—**direct and contextual**—affect the quality and specificity of AI responses.

- **Direct prompts** request a simple response, often concise and fact-based.
- **Contextual prompts** provide additional background, guiding AI to generate a more **relevant, detailed, and tailored** response.

Both approaches are valuable, depending on the **goal, complexity, and required accuracy** of the output.

Understanding Direct Prompts

What Are Direct Prompts?

Direct prompts are straightforward, **concise queries or commands**. They do not include additional context or instructions beyond the essential request.

- Suitable for **fact-based answers**
- Effective for **quick responses**
- Used for **simple tasks or broad overviews**

Examples of Direct Prompts

Direct Prompt	AI Expected Response

"What is machine learning?"	Provides a **brief definition**.
"List three benefits of remote work."	Offers a **short list**.
"Translate 'Hello' into Spanish."	Returns **'Hola'**.
"Summarize World War II."	Gives a **general historical overview**.
"Generate a Python function for sorting a list."	Produces a **basic sorting algorithm**.

While direct prompts **quickly provide answers**, they may **lack depth, nuance, or customization** if a topic requires **analysis, comparison, or industry-specific information**.

Understanding Contextual Prompts

What Are Contextual Prompts?

Contextual prompts add **specific details, instructions, or guiding elements** to refine the AI's response.

- **Enhances clarity** by setting expectations for output.
- **Improves accuracy** by narrowing the response scope.
- **Personalizes responses** based on industry, audience, or purpose.

Examples of Contextual Prompts

Contextual Prompt	AI Expected Response
"Explain machine learning with examples from healthcare."	Provides a **detailed response with industry-specific examples**.
"List three benefits of remote work, focusing on productivity and work-life balance."	Offers **a refined, targeted list** based on specified areas.
"Translate 'Hello' into Spanish and French, and explain pronunciation."	Returns **'Hola' and 'Bonjour' with pronunciation guides**.
"Summarize World War II, focusing on its impact on global politics."	Generates **a political analysis of the war's consequences**.
"Generate a Python function for sorting a list, optimized for large datasets."	Produces **an advanced sorting algorithm (e.g., QuickSort or MergeSort)**.

Contextual prompts ensure **more relevant and specialized** responses by **framing the AI's approach**.

Comparing Direct vs. Contextual Prompts

Feature	Direct Prompts	Contextual Prompts
Detail Level	Basic, general	Comprehensive, tailored
Response Depth	Brief	In-depth
Use Case	Quick facts, simple tasks	Complex topics, nuanced insights
Example	"Explain blockchain."	"Explain blockchain and its role in decentralized finance."
AI Adaptability	Limited	High

Examples in Different Contexts

Business Context

Direct Prompt:

"How do businesses use AI?"
AI Response:
"Businesses use AI for automation, data analysis, and customer service."

Contextual Prompt:

"How do businesses in the retail industry use AI to enhance customer experience?"
 AI Response:
 *"Retail businesses use AI for **personalized recommendations, customer chatbots**, and **supply chain optimization**. AI-driven analytics track customer behavior to improve shopping experiences and increase sales efficiency."*

Healthcare Context

Direct Prompt:

"What is telemedicine?"
 AI Response:
 "Telemedicine is the use of technology to provide remote healthcare services."

Contextual Prompt:

"Explain how telemedicine has improved healthcare access in rural areas."
 AI Response:
 *"Telemedicine has significantly **expanded healthcare access in rural areas** by providing **remote consultations**, reducing the need for travel, and enabling **faster diagnosis** for patients who lack access to specialists. It is particularly beneficial for **chronic disease management and mental health services**."*

Technical Context

Direct Prompt:

"What is an API?"
 AI Response:
 "An API (Application Programming Interface) is a set of protocols that allow software applications to communicate."

Contextual Prompt:

"Explain RESTful APIs and how they differ from SOAP APIs."
 AI Response:
 *"A **RESTful API** follows REST (Representational State Transfer) principles and communicates over **HTTP using standard methods** like GET, POST, PUT, and*
35

*DELETE. It is **lightweight, scalable, and widely used for web services**. In contrast, **SOAP (Simple Object Access Protocol) APIs** use XML messaging and are considered **more secure but heavier in data processing**."*

When to Use Direct vs. Contextual Prompts

Scenario	Best Approach	Example Prompt
Looking for a simple fact	Direct	"What year did the Titanic sink?"
Seeking a quick definition	Direct	"Define quantum computing."
Requiring depth and analysis	Contextual	"Explain quantum computing and its potential applications in cybersecurity."
Writing professional content	Contextual	"Generate a blog post on AI in education, focusing on personalized learning."
Generating creative outputs	Contextual	"Write a short sci-fi story set in a future

		where AI governs human society."

Best Practices for Effective Prompting

1. **Use direct prompts for quick, factual responses.**
2. **Use contextual prompts when depth, personalization, or industry relevance is needed.**
3. **Specify the purpose or intended audience for better-targeted AI responses.**
4. **Incorporate details such as timeframe, constraints, or examples for refinement.**
5. **Iterate and refine prompts based on AI-generated results.**

By understanding and applying **direct and contextual prompting techniques**, users can significantly enhance **AI efficiency, response accuracy, and overall interaction quality**.

Role-Based Prompting for Specific Outputs

Artificial intelligence models do not inherently possess **role awareness** or expertise in any specific domain. However, **role-based prompting** enables AI to **simulate expertise** by defining its **persona, knowledge scope, and response style**. This technique significantly enhances the **accuracy, tone, and structure of AI-generated responses** by guiding the model to **think and respond** as if it were an expert in a given field.

Understanding Role-Based Prompting

Role-based prompting assigns the AI a **specific identity or profession** before requesting a response. This method helps **fine-tune AI behavior, response depth, and language style**, ensuring that the output aligns with **industry standards, academic expectations, or professional requirements**.

For example, instead of asking:

- "Explain blockchain technology."

A role-based prompt refines the request:

- "You are a blockchain expert explaining the fundamentals of blockchain technology to an audience of finance professionals. Use real-world examples and technical insights."

By incorporating **role-playing elements**, AI produces responses **tailored to the assigned identity**, significantly improving clarity, structure, and domain relevance.

Examples of Role-Based Prompting for Different Fields

1. **Technical and Scientific Explanations**

   - "You are a data scientist. Explain machine learning algorithms for predictive analytics in business applications."
   - "You are a medical researcher. Describe how AI is used in cancer diagnostics, referencing recent advancements."

2. **Content Writing and Copywriting**

   - "You are a professional copywriter. Write a persuasive product description for a smartwatch targeting fitness enthusiasts."
   - "You are a journalist writing a news article on climate change policies in Europe."

3. **Education and Training**

   - "You are a university professor teaching an introductory Python programming course. Explain object-oriented programming with examples."
   - "You are an elementary school teacher. Explain the concept of photosynthesis to a 10-year-old using simple terms."

4. **Legal and Compliance Guidance**

   - "You are a corporate lawyer. Draft a business partnership agreement outlining rights and responsibilities."
   - "You are a GDPR consultant. Explain the key principles of data protection for a SaaS startup."

5. **Business and Marketing Strategies**

   - "You are a business strategist. Provide five growth strategies for a small e-commerce startup looking to expand internationally."

    ◦ "You are a digital marketing expert. Outline an SEO strategy for a new online fashion brand."

6. **Creative Writing and Storytelling**

    ◦ "You are a screenwriter. Write an opening scene for a thriller movie set in a dystopian future."
    ◦ "You are a historical novelist. Write a dialogue exchange between Leonardo da Vinci and Michelangelo debating art techniques."

Role-based prompting **enhances AI-generated responses** by aligning them with **professional standards, industry terminology, and expected knowledge depth**. By **assigning an identity**, users can achieve **greater precision and relevance** in AI-generated content.

Using Constraints to Guide AI Responses

AI models operate by **predicting the most probable sequence of words**, which means that **open-ended or broad prompts** can lead to **unfocused, lengthy, or off-topic responses**. **Using constraints** in a prompt helps **narrow AI output**, ensuring that responses are **concise, structured, and aligned with user expectations**.

Understanding Constraints in Prompt Engineering

Constraints are **guidelines, boundaries, or limitations** embedded in a prompt to **control the length, format, style, and specificity** of AI responses. They help in:

- Preventing AI from **going off-topic** or providing excessive information.
- Ensuring AI-generated content **fits within predefined parameters**.
- Directing AI to **follow structured formats**, such as lists, tables, or step-by-step explanations.

Types of Constraints in Prompt Engineering

39

1. Word Count and Length Constraints

Setting **word or sentence limits** ensures that AI **provides a concise response** without unnecessary elaboration.

- **Without Constraints:** "Summarize the history of artificial intelligence."
- **With Constraints:** "Summarize the history of artificial intelligence in 150 words, focusing on key milestones and breakthroughs."

Adding a **word limit** makes the AI **prioritize relevant points** and avoid excessive detail.

2. Formatting Constraints

Specifying a **desired format** ensures that AI **delivers structured responses** in an easy-to-read manner.

- **Without Constraints:** "Explain how photosynthesis works."
- **With Constraints:** "Explain how photosynthesis works in bullet points, covering the role of sunlight, chlorophyll, and carbon dioxide."

By defining a format, AI generates a **structured and organized response**.

3. Style and Tone Constraints

AI can adjust responses to match **formal, casual, persuasive, or technical writing styles**.

- **Without Constraints:** "Write an article about electric vehicles."
- **With Constraints:** "Write a professional, data-driven article about the benefits of electric vehicles, citing industry statistics."

The constraint **modifies the tone** to align with **professional and research-based writing styles**.

4. Scope Constraints

Scope constraints **define boundaries** to keep AI focused on **a particular aspect of a topic**.

- **Without Constraints:** "Explain the impact of artificial intelligence."
- **With Constraints:** "Explain the impact of artificial intelligence in healthcare, specifically focusing on medical imaging and diagnostics."

40

The AI will **stay within the given scope**, making the response **more targeted and relevant**.

5. Logical and Step-by-Step Constraints

AI can be **instructed to explain concepts in sequential steps**, improving clarity.

- **Without Constraints:** "Explain how a neural network works."
- **With Constraints:** "Explain how a neural network works in five steps, using simple language suitable for a beginner in AI."

By guiding AI through **step-by-step logic**, responses become **more accessible and structured**.

Benefits of Using Constraints

- **Eliminates ambiguity**, ensuring **direct, to-the-point answers**.
- **Reduces response unpredictability**, avoiding **unnecessary details or off-topic information**.
- **Improves response structure**, making content **easier to read and understand**.
- **Optimizes AI usability**, particularly in business, research, and technical writing scenarios.

By **embedding constraints in prompts**, AI-generated responses become **more aligned with user expectations**, leading to **high-quality, tailored outputs**.

Table: Types of Basic Prompts and Expected Outputs

Prompt Type	Description	Example Prompt	Expected Output
Open-ended Prompt	Provides broad, general responses. Best for exploratory discussions.	"Tell me about artificial intelligence."	AI generates **a general explanation**, covering multiple aspects of AI.

Guided Prompt	Directs AI toward a **specific focus area** within a topic.	"Explain artificial intelligence, focusing on its role in self-driving cars."	AI **narrows the response** to discuss AI in self-driving vehicles.
Role-Bas ed Prompt	Assigns the AI a **specific identity or expertise**.	"You are a cybersecurity expert. Explain the importance of multi-factor authentication."	AI **mimics an expert**, providing **in-depth, technical insights**.
Comparat ive Prompt	Asks AI to **compare two or more subjects**.	"Compare Python and JavaScript for backend development."	AI **contrasts both languages**, outlining key similarities and differences.
Constrain t-Based Prompt	Restricts AI response based on **length, format, or scope**.	"Summarize blockchain technology in 200 words."	AI **delivers a structured, concise summary**.
Step-by-S tep Prompt	Instructs AI to **break down a complex topic into sequential steps**.	"Explain how a neural network works in five steps."	AI **structures the response logically**, making it easy to follow.

Basic prompt types lay the foundation for **effective AI interaction**, ensuring **clear, structured, and purpose-driven responses**. By combining role-based prompting with constraints, users can **maximize AI efficiency and precision** across diverse applications.

Chapter 5

Chain-of-Thought Prompting

Why Breaking Down Steps Improves Accuracy

Artificial intelligence models operate based on **probability-driven text generation**, meaning they predict the most likely next token (word or phrase) based on the input provided. However, when presented with complex queries, AI **may not always reason effectively** or provide accurate and logical responses. This is where **Chain-of-Thought (CoT) prompting** becomes crucial.

Chain-of-Thought prompting is a **method used to improve AI reasoning by breaking down complex tasks into step-by-step instructions**. Instead of expecting the AI to generate an answer immediately, **CoT prompts guide AI through a structured, logical thought process**, significantly enhancing accuracy, depth, and coherence.

How Breaking Down Steps Enhances AI Responses

1. **Improves Logical Consistency**
   AI models **do not inherently reason like humans** but instead rely on patterns from training data. When provided with **a step-by-step breakdown**, the AI **logically follows** each part of the problem instead of jumping to conclusions.

   - **Without CoT Prompting:** "What is 27 × 13?" → AI may provide an **instant numerical answer**.
   - **With CoT Prompting:** "Solve 27 × 13 step by step, first breaking it into (27 × 10) + (27 × 3)." → AI **follows a structured multiplication process**, ensuring greater accuracy.

2. **Enhances Problem-Solving Abilities**
   AI models can struggle with **multi-step reasoning tasks**, especially in areas like **math, science, and programming**. CoT prompting forces the model to **work through each component of the problem**, ensuring the final answer is **logically derived** rather than **statistically guessed**.

   - **Example Without CoT:** "Find the square root of 144 and then add 10."

- Example With CoT:
    - "First, find the square root of 144."
    - "Next, add 10 to your result."
    - "Now, state the final answer."
3. By instructing AI to **process each step sequentially**, it significantly reduces **computation errors**.

4. **Reduces AI Hallucination and Misinterpretation**
   AI models sometimes **generate incorrect, misleading, or fabricated answers** (known as hallucinations). A **stepwise prompt structure** helps AI **verify each part of the reasoning process**, reducing the chance of hallucination.

    - **Example Without CoT:** "Explain why the sun sets in the east." → AI might **fabricate information** instead of correcting the premise.
    - **Example With CoT:**
        - "First, explain Earth's rotation."
        - "Next, describe how Earth's rotation affects the position of the sun."
        - "Now, state whether the sun sets in the east or west and correct any misconceptions."
5. The **stepwise approach forces AI to fact-check and provide accurate answers**.

6. **Improves AI's Ability to Handle Complex Queries**
   AI models often **truncate or simplify responses** when handling **long, multi-faceted queries**. By breaking the question into smaller parts, CoT prompting ensures **each component is fully addressed**.

    - **Example Without CoT:** "Explain how photosynthesis works, its chemical reactions, and its importance to ecosystems." → AI **may summarize briefly**, missing key details.
    - **Example With CoT:**
        - "Explain the process of photosynthesis, including light absorption."
        - "Describe the chemical reactions, including carbon fixation and oxygen release."
        - "Explain why photosynthesis is crucial for sustaining ecosystems."
7. This **ensures a well-structured, comprehensive response**.

8. **Mimics Human Problem-Solving Methods**
   Humans **naturally approach complex problems step by step**—whether solving a math equation, debugging a program, or writing an essay. AI functions more effectively when following **structured thinking patterns**.

   - **Example:**
     - A human writing an essay starts with an **outline, thesis statement, body paragraphs, and conclusion**.
     - AI will generate **better content** if prompted to **construct each section separately**, rather than generating an entire essay in one go.

Breaking down steps helps AI **emulate human logical processing**, leading to **higher-quality, well-reasoned responses**.

Designing Multi-Step Prompts for Logical Responses

A well-designed **multi-step prompt** ensures that AI follows a **structured approach** to problem-solving, reducing errors and improving response quality. The process involves **breaking down a query into manageable sub-tasks**, allowing AI to reason **systematically rather than reactively**.

Key Components of a Multi-Step Prompt

A good **multi-step prompt** includes:

1. **A clear breakdown of logical steps**
2. **Stepwise processing for accurate results**
3. **Guided sequencing to prevent AI shortcuts**
4. **Explicit instructions to ensure structured output**

To design an effective **multi-step prompt**, follow these principles:

1. Define the Problem in Sequential Steps

Instead of asking AI for an immediate answer, **guide it through the thinking process step by step**.

- **Poor Prompt:** "Explain how airplanes fly."
- **Effective Multi-Step Prompt:**
    1. "Explain the four forces acting on an airplane: lift, thrust, drag, and gravity."
    2. "Describe how Bernoulli's principle and airfoil shape contribute to lift."
    3. "Summarize how jet engines generate thrust."
    4. "Explain how pilots control an airplane's altitude and direction."

Breaking the explanation into **logical steps ensures** that AI **does not omit important details**.

2. Use Step-by-Step Numbering or Bullet Points

When designing prompts, explicitly **number the steps or use bullet points** to ensure **structured responses**.

- **Without Numbering:** "Describe how a computer processes information, including input, processing, storage, and output." → AI may mix up steps or omit key details.
- **With Numbering:**
    1. "Describe how data enters a computer via input devices."
    2. "Explain how the CPU processes data using logic gates and memory."
    3. "Describe how data is stored temporarily and permanently."
    4. "Explain how the output is generated and displayed on a screen."

Using **numbered sequences** makes AI **follow a logical thought process**, avoiding confusion.

3. Request AI to Justify Each Step

In critical thinking scenarios, ask AI to **explain each decision** before proceeding.

- **Poor Prompt:** "Explain why renewable energy is important." → AI might **list reasons without in-depth analysis**.
- **Effective Multi-Step Prompt:**
    1. "Define renewable energy and its types (solar, wind, hydro, geothermal)."
    2. "Explain the environmental benefits of renewable energy over fossil fuels."

3. "Analyze how renewable energy reduces carbon emissions and contributes to climate goals."
4. "Discuss economic and technological challenges in implementing renewable energy."

By instructing AI to **justify each point**, the response **becomes more structured and logical**.

4. Prevent AI from Skipping Steps

AI sometimes **attempts to provide immediate conclusions** without detailing the reasoning process. To prevent this, **explicitly state that AI must complete each step before moving forward**.

- **Example:**
    - "Solve the equation 3x + 5 = 20 step by step.
        1. First, isolate the variable x.
        2. Then, divide both sides by the appropriate coefficient.
        3. Finally, verify the solution."

This prevents AI from **skipping the middle steps** and ensures **structured problem-solving**.

5. Encourage AI to Think Critically

For **subjective or analytical tasks**, guide AI to **consider multiple perspectives** before concluding.

- **Example:**
    - "Analyze the impact of artificial intelligence on the job market.
        1. Discuss industries most affected by automation.
        2. Explain how AI creates new job opportunities.
        3. Evaluate whether AI-driven job displacement outweighs job creation.
        4. Summarize the long-term societal impact of AI on employment."

This approach **forces AI to consider multiple viewpoints**, improving the depth of its responses.

Multi-step prompts **enhance AI's reasoning**, ensure **logical consistency**, and lead to **better-structured, more reliable responses**. By breaking complex tasks into

manageable steps, AI can process and generate answers **with greater accuracy and depth**, ultimately making it a more powerful tool for problem-solving.

Real-World Examples of Chain-of-Thought Prompting

Chain-of-Thought (CoT) prompting is highly effective across various **real-world applications**, improving AI's ability to **reason logically, break down complex problems, and generate structured outputs**. Below are **practical examples** demonstrating the benefits of CoT prompting across different domains, including **mathematics, programming, business strategy, medical diagnosis, and creative writing**.

---

1. Mathematics: Solving a Complex Problem Step by Step

AI often struggles with **multi-step mathematical problems** if asked to provide an answer in a single step. Chain-of-Thought prompting improves accuracy by forcing AI to **explain its reasoning sequentially**.

- **Simple Prompt (Without CoT)**

    - *"Solve 243 × 12."*
    - AI may immediately generate an answer **without showing calculations**, leading to potential errors.
- **Chain-of-Thought Prompt**

    - *"Solve 243 × 12 step by step. Break it down into smaller calculations before providing the final result."*
    - AI Response:
        1. Break 243 × 12 into (243 × 10) + (243 × 2).
        2. 243 × 10 = 2430.
        3. 243 × 2 = 486.
        4. Add 2430 + 486 = **2916**.

- The **stepwise approach** ensures AI does **not skip calculations**, reducing computational errors.

---

2. Programming: Debugging Code Effectively

When debugging code, AI can make **more reliable suggestions** if guided through a **structured thought process**.

- **Simple Prompt (Without CoT)**

  - *"Fix this Python error: TypeError: unsupported operand type(s) for +: 'int' and 'str'."*
  - AI may generate a **generic answer**, assuming an incorrect variable conversion.
- **Chain-of-Thought Prompt**

  - *"Analyze the error step by step:

    1. Identify which line of code is causing the issue.
    2. Explain why the TypeError is occurring.
    3. Suggest a way to fix the issue with proper type conversion."*
  - AI Response:

    1. The error occurs when attempting to add an integer and a string.
    2. This happens because Python does not support direct addition between different data types.
    3. Solution: Convert the integer to a string using `str()` or convert the string to an integer using `int()`.
  - By **forcing AI to break down the debugging process**, the output is **more detailed and tailored to the actual problem**.

3. Business Strategy: Developing a Marketing Plan

In business decision-making, AI can **improve strategic recommendations** when prompted to **analyze situations sequentially**.

- **Simple Prompt (Without CoT)**

  - *"Suggest a marketing strategy for a new fitness app."*

49

- AI may provide **generic marketing tips** without considering **market positioning, audience targeting, and campaign execution**.
- **Chain-of-Thought Prompt**

  - *"Develop a marketing strategy for a new fitness app by following these steps:

    1. Identify the target audience.
    2. Define the unique value proposition.
    3. Outline online and offline marketing strategies.
    4. Suggest performance metrics to track success."*
  - AI Response:

    1. **Target Audience:** Health-conscious individuals, young professionals, and gym-goers.
    2. **Value Proposition:** AI-driven personalized workouts and meal tracking.
    3. **Marketing Strategy:**
       - Online: Social media ads, influencer collaborations, content marketing.
       - Offline: Partnerships with gyms, local fitness events.
    4. **Performance Metrics:** User sign-ups, app engagement, and conversion rates.
  - The **stepwise breakdown** ensures AI provides **a structured and actionable marketing strategy**.

4. Medical Diagnosis: Assisting Healthcare Professionals

In healthcare applications, AI can generate **more accurate and structured diagnostic reasoning** when guided through a **logical sequence**.

- **Simple Prompt (Without CoT)**

  - *"Diagnose a patient with fatigue and shortness of breath."*
  - AI may **instantly suggest** common causes like **anemia or respiratory issues** but overlook other possibilities.
- **Chain-of-Thought Prompt**

  - *"Analyze this medical case step by step:

    1. Identify possible causes of fatigue and shortness of breath.
    2. Ask relevant diagnostic questions.

3. Suggest preliminary tests for accurate diagnosis.
4. Provide potential treatment recommendations."*

- AI Response:

  1. **Possible Causes:** Anemia, heart disease, chronic obstructive pulmonary disease (COPD), anxiety disorders.
  2. **Diagnostic Questions:**
     - How long has the patient experienced symptoms?
     - Are there additional symptoms (chest pain, dizziness, or weight loss)?
  3. **Recommended Tests:** Complete blood count (CBC), ECG, pulmonary function test.
  4. **Possible Treatment Plans:** Based on test results, treatments may range from iron supplementation to cardiology consultation.

- This approach ensures AI **thoroughly evaluates** all possible scenarios before providing an answer.

5. Creative Writing: Generating a Story with a Logical Flow

When using AI for **creative storytelling**, structuring the prompt **in multiple steps** results in **better coherence and plot development**.

- **Simple Prompt (Without CoT)**

  - *"Write a short sci-fi story about time travel."*
  - AI may generate **a random sequence of events** without logical consistency.
- **Chain-of-Thought Prompt**

  - *"Generate a sci-fi story using the following structure:

    1. Introduce the main character and setting.
    2. Describe how they discover the time travel mechanism.
    3. Explain the consequences of their first time-travel attempt.
    4. Develop a conflict related to time paradoxes.
    5. Resolve the story with an unexpected twist."*
  - AI Response (Excerpt):

    1. **Introduction:** Dr. Ava Carter, a quantum physicist, discovers an ancient device buried in Antarctica.

2. **Discovery:** The device allows time travel but only in **10-year increments**.
3. **First Travel Attempt:** She jumps to 2050 and sees Earth ravaged by climate disasters.
4. **Conflict:** Her actions in the past unknowingly triggered the catastrophe.
5. **Resolution:** She must decide between **destroying the time machine** or **rewriting history at great personal cost**.
   - By **structuring the storytelling process**, AI maintains coherence, **character development, and logical progression**.

Illustration: Flowchart of Chain-of-Thought Prompting

To visually represent how **CoT prompting** improves AI reasoning, the following flowchart outlines **how AI processes multi-step logical reasoning tasks**:

plaintext
CopyEdit

```
        +---------------------------------------+
        | User Input: Multi-Step Problem        |
        +---------------------------------------+
                          |
                          v
        +---------------------------------------+
        | Step 1: Identify the Core Problem     |
        +---------------------------------------+
                          |
                          v
        +---------------------------------------+
        | Step 2: Break Down into Subtasks      |
        | (Define logical steps)                |
        +---------------------------------------+
                          |
```

```
                      v
+---------------------------------------+
| Step 3: Process Each Step Sequentially|
| (Ensure logical consistency)          |
+---------------------------------------+
                |
                v
+---------------------------------------+
| Step 4: Verify and Refine the Output  |
| (Ensure factual accuracy)             |
+---------------------------------------+
                |
                v
+---------------------------------------+
| AI Generates a Coherent Response      |
+---------------------------------------+
```

This flowchart **demonstrates** how AI **approaches complex queries using a structured, step-by-step reasoning process**, ensuring **higher accuracy and improved logical consistency**.

By applying **Chain-of-Thought prompting**, users can significantly **improve AI-generated responses** across a wide range of **technical, creative, and analytical applications**.

Chapter 6

Zero-Shot, Few-Shot, and Multi-Shot Prompting

Understanding Zero-Shot Prompting for Unfamiliar Tasks

What is Zero-Shot Prompting?

Zero-shot prompting refers to the ability of an AI model to **perform a task without prior examples or contextual training within the prompt**. This technique relies on the model's **pre-existing knowledge**, learned from extensive training data, to generate responses for tasks it has never explicitly encountered before.

In a zero-shot prompt, the AI is given **only the instruction** with no examples to guide its response. The model must rely entirely on its ability to infer meaning, apply learned patterns, and predict an appropriate output **without additional context**.

Why Zero-Shot Prompting is Important

Zero-shot prompting is useful because:

- It **saves time** by allowing AI to handle queries instantly without requiring additional input examples.
- It enables AI to generalize knowledge across **different domains**.
- It is practical when there is **no reference data** available for comparison.
- It can be applied to a **wide range of tasks**, from simple fact retrieval to complex reasoning.

Examples of Zero-Shot Prompting in Different Fields

1. General Knowledge Retrieval

- **Prompt:** "What is the capital of Canada?"
- **AI Response:** "The capital of Canada is Ottawa."

Since factual knowledge is stored within the AI model's training data, it can **retrieve and generate answers instantly**.

2. Text Summarization

- **Prompt:** "Summarize the following article in one paragraph: [Insert article text]."
- **AI Response:** The AI attempts to summarize the content **without prior examples of how the summary should be structured**.

3. Language Translation

- **Prompt:** "Translate the following sentence into Spanish: 'Good morning, how are you today?'"
- **AI Response:** "Buenos días, ¿cómo estás hoy?"

Even though no examples were provided in the prompt, the AI **leverages its training data** to infer an accurate translation.

4. Sentiment Analysis

- **Prompt:** "Analyze the sentiment of this review: 'The service was slow, and the food was cold.'"
- **AI Response:** "Negative sentiment."

The AI correctly classifies sentiment **without prior exposure to similar examples in the prompt**.

Challenges of Zero-Shot Prompting

Despite its usefulness, zero-shot prompting has limitations:

1. **Lower Accuracy in Complex Tasks** – Without examples, AI may **misinterpret** the desired response format.
2. **Lack of Contextual Understanding** – AI relies on generalizations and might **overlook nuances**.
3. **Higher Risk of Errors in Unfamiliar Scenarios** – AI's training data **may not fully cover niche topics**, leading to **less reliable answers**.

Example of a Zero-Shot Prompt Producing an Incorrect Response

- **Prompt:** "Generate a Python script that scrapes product reviews from an e-commerce website."

- **Possible AI Mistake:** AI may produce a script **without handling anti-scraping measures** (like CAPTCHAs), leading to incomplete results.

To improve **accuracy and reliability, few-shot learning** can be leveraged.

Leveraging Few-Shot Learning to Improve AI Accuracy

What is Few-Shot Prompting?

Few-shot prompting enhances AI performance by **providing one or more examples** within the prompt. These examples **demonstrate the expected output format,** guiding AI **toward more accurate and contextually relevant responses**.

Few-shot learning helps AI models **adapt to new tasks** by **learning from minimal examples** instead of requiring extensive fine-tuning.

Why Few-Shot Prompting is Effective

Few-shot learning improves AI responses by:

- **Reducing ambiguity** and guiding AI toward the correct output.
- **Enhancing accuracy in complex or nuanced tasks** where zero-shot responses may be unreliable.
- **Ensuring AI follows specific formatting and style expectations**.
- **Minimizing response variability** by reinforcing structured patterns.

Examples of Few-Shot Prompting in Different Fields

1. Text Classification

Instead of asking AI to classify sentiment without any reference, **few-shot learning provides examples**.

- **Prompt:**

- "Classify the sentiment of the following reviews as 'Positive' or 'Negative':
    - Review: 'I love this product! It works perfectly.' → Sentiment: Positive
    - Review: 'The quality is terrible. Do not buy.' → Sentiment: Negative
    - Review: 'The service was slow, and the food was cold.' → Sentiment: ?"
- **AI Response:** "Negative"

Providing examples **trains AI to recognize sentiment patterns** before generating its own classification.

---

2. Code Generation and Debugging

Few-shot learning improves AI's ability to **write and debug code effectively**.

- **Prompt:**

"Here's how to write a function to add two numbers:
python
CopyEdit

```
def add_numbers(a, b):
    return a + b
```

- Now write a function to multiply two numbers."

AI Response:
python
CopyEdit

```
def multiply_numbers(a, b):
    return a * b
```

-

By **demonstrating a pattern** (addition function), AI **accurately applies the logic** to multiplication.

---

3. Customer Support Response Formatting

Few-shot prompting can **ensure AI-generated responses match a specific communication style**.

- **Prompt:**
    - "Respond to customer inquiries using the following format:
        - Inquiry: 'I received the wrong product. What should I do?'
          Response: 'We're sorry for the mix-up! Please contact our support team at [email] with your order details, and we'll send the correct product immediately.'
        - Inquiry: 'The item I received is defective.'
          Response: ?"
- **AI Response:**
    - "We're sorry for the inconvenience! Please reach out to our support team at [email] with a description of the issue, and we'll arrange a replacement for you."

This **ensures AI maintains brand tone and structured responses**.

---

4. Complex Logical Reasoning

Few-shot learning helps AI **analyze problems more systematically**, especially in logical or technical domains.

- **Prompt:**
    - "Solve the following algebra problems step by step:
        - Problem: $2x + 3 = 9$
          Step 1: Subtract 3 from both sides → $2x = 6$
          Step 2: Divide by 2 → $x = 3$
        - Problem: $5x - 7 = 18$
          Step 1: ?"
- **AI Response:**
    - "Add 7 to both sides → $5x = 25$
      Divide by 5 → $x = 5$"

Providing one example **teaches AI to apply the same method** to new problems.

How to Design an Effective Few-Shot Prompt

To maximize accuracy in AI responses, few-shot prompts should include:

1. **Clear examples** – Show AI the expected input-output relationship.
2. **Consistent patterns** – Ensure all examples follow the same structure.
3. **Gradual complexity scaling** – Start with simple cases, then introduce more challenging ones.
4. **Explicit formatting instructions** – Guide AI in following the correct style or structure.

Comparison: Zero-Shot vs. Few-Shot Prompting

Criteria	Zero-Shot Prompting	Few-Shot Prompting
Definition	AI generates responses without examples.	AI is provided with a few examples to learn from.
Accuracy	Lower for complex tasks.	Higher due to contextual guidance.
Suitability	Best for simple, factual queries.	Best for complex, structured responses.
Response Consistency	May vary significantly.	More stable and predictable.
Context Awareness	Limited, relies on general knowledge.	Learns from given examples to improve relevance.

Few-shot learning significantly **reduces the risk of AI errors and inconsistencies**, making it ideal for **tasks requiring structured, logical, or domain-specific knowledge**.

Few-shot prompting enhances **AI accuracy, contextual awareness, and response structure**, ensuring **more reliable and professional outputs**. By **guiding AI with well-chosen examples**, users can optimize **task-specific AI performance** and **minimize misinterpretations in complex problem-solving scenarios**.

Chapter 7

Systematic Prompt Refinement

How to Evaluate and Improve Prompt Responses

Artificial intelligence models, particularly large language models (LLMs), **do not inherently understand intent** in the way humans do. Instead, they **generate responses based on statistical probabilities**, which means that **small changes in a prompt can lead to significant differences in output quality**. To achieve the most **relevant, accurate, and structured responses**, it is essential to **evaluate and refine prompts systematically**.

Why Prompt Evaluation Matters

Prompt responses must be **evaluated and improved continuously** because:

1. **AI-generated content can be inconsistent**, producing **varying levels of accuracy and relevance**.
2. The same **prompt may yield different results** depending on the **context and phrasing**.
3. AI **may misinterpret intent** if the prompt is ambiguous or lacks clarity.
4. **Real-world applications**, such as business, coding, education, and research, require **precise, structured outputs** that AI must consistently generate.

Criteria for Evaluating Prompt Effectiveness

A **well-structured prompt** should produce responses that meet the following criteria:

1. **Accuracy**

   - Does the response correctly address the question or task?
   - Are there **factual errors, misunderstandings, or missing details**?
   - **Example:**
     - **Weak Response:** "The Eiffel Tower is in Berlin."
     - **Strong Response:** "The Eiffel Tower is in Paris, France. It was completed in 1889 and is a famous cultural landmark."

2. **Relevance**

   - Does the response align with the **intended purpose of the prompt**?
   - Is **extraneous or off-topic information** included?
   - **Example:**
     - **Weak Response:** Asking for "the impact of artificial intelligence in healthcare" but receiving information about AI in gaming.

3. **Completeness**

   - Does the response **fully answer the prompt**?
   - Is there **missing context, insufficient details, or an incomplete explanation**?
   - **Example:**
     - **Incomplete Prompt:** "Explain photosynthesis."
     - **Optimized Prompt:** "Explain the process of photosynthesis, including the role of light, chlorophyll, and carbon dioxide in plant energy production."

4. **Conciseness**

   - Is the response **too verbose or too brief**?
   - Does AI provide **unnecessary information** that dilutes the main point?
   - **Example:**
     - **Weak Response:** Overloading a simple answer with **excessive technical jargon** when a simplified explanation is needed.

5. **Logical Coherence and Organization**

   - Does the response **follow a logical order**, making it easy to understand?
   - Are **key points clearly structured**?
   - **Example:**
     - **Unstructured Answer:** A disorganized paragraph explaining **machine learning, artificial intelligence, and deep learning without distinction**.
     - **Refined Answer:** A **clear breakdown**, explaining AI as a broader field, ML as a subset of AI, and deep learning as a more advanced ML technique.

6. **Format Adherence**

- If a specific format is requested, does AI **follow the requested structure**?
- Examples include **lists, tables, bullet points, paragraph summaries, or step-by-step explanations**.
- **Example:**
  - **Weak Response:** A long paragraph when asked for **bullet points**.
  - **Optimized Prompt:** "List five key features of Python programming using bullet points."

Methods to Improve Prompt Responses

Once an AI-generated response has been **evaluated**, **refining the prompt** helps improve accuracy. Some techniques for improving prompts include:

1. Rewriting for Clarity and Specificity

If the AI response is **too general or ambiguous**, rephrase the prompt to **eliminate vagueness**.

- **Original Prompt:** "Tell me about renewable energy." (Too broad)
- **Refined Prompt:** "Explain the main types of renewable energy (solar, wind, hydro, geothermal) and their environmental benefits."

2. Adding Context for Precision

AI models generate better responses **when they understand the full context**.

- **Original Prompt:** "Explain Newton's Laws of Motion." (Generic response)
- **Refined Prompt:** "Explain Newton's Three Laws of Motion, including examples from everyday life and their application in vehicle safety."

3. Using Constraints to Limit or Expand Responses

Setting word limits, defining scope, or specifying response length improves **response focus**.

- **Original Prompt:** "Summarize the impact of the Industrial Revolution." (Unclear scope)
- **Refined Prompt:** "Summarize the impact of the Industrial Revolution in 200 words, focusing on technological advancements and economic effects."

4. Requesting a Step-by-Step Breakdown

For complex topics, breaking down information **improves response structure and logical consistency**.

- **Original Prompt:** "Explain how machine learning works."
- **Refined Prompt:** "Explain how machine learning works step by step, covering data collection, model training, evaluation, and real-world applications."

5. Specifying Format Preferences

AI responds better when given **clear formatting instructions**.

- **Original Prompt:** "List the benefits of cloud computing." (May return in paragraph form)
- **Refined Prompt:** "List the five key benefits of cloud computing using bullet points, each with a brief explanation."

6. Iterative Testing for Refinement

Testing and adjusting prompts helps **fine-tune AI responses** over multiple iterations.

- **First Attempt:** "Explain AI in business." → AI response is too broad.
- **Second Attempt:** "Explain how AI improves efficiency in business, focusing on automation, data analysis, and customer service." → More precise.
- **Third Attempt:** "Provide three case studies of AI improving business efficiency in retail, healthcare, and banking." → AI response now includes real-world applications.

Each refinement **improves AI's ability to generate useful responses**, reducing ambiguity and enhancing precision.

Iterative Adjustments for Better Accuracy

What is Iterative Prompt Adjustment?

Iterative adjustment involves **modifying a prompt multiple times** based on **AI output quality**. Instead of expecting a perfect response on the first attempt, **each iteration refines the prompt** to better guide AI behavior.

Step-by-Step Process for Iterative Prompt Adjustment

1. **Generate an Initial Response**

   o Use a **basic version of the prompt** and assess AI output.
2. **Identify Weaknesses** in AI Output

   o Look for **gaps in accuracy, relevance, or formatting issues**.
3. **Modify the Prompt for Clarity**

   o Add **specific constraints, formatting requirements, or contextual details**.
4. **Test the New Prompt**

   o Run the modified prompt again and evaluate improvements.
5. **Repeat Until Desired Accuracy is Achieved**

   o Continue refining the prompt **until AI consistently produces high-quality responses**.

Example of Iterative Refinement in Practice

Scenario: Generating an AI-Optimized Business Strategy

1. **First Attempt:**

   o **Prompt:** "How can a company improve online sales?"
   o **Issue:** AI response is **too broad** and covers generic suggestions.
2. **Second Attempt (Refined Prompt):**

   o **Prompt:** "How can an e-commerce company increase online sales? Focus on digital marketing, SEO, and customer engagement strategies."
   o **Improvement:** AI now **focuses on e-commerce** but still lacks **real-world examples**.
3. **Third Attempt (Further Refinement):**

   o **Prompt:** "How can an e-commerce company increase online sales? Provide three case studies where digital marketing, SEO, or customer engagement significantly improved revenue."
   o **Final Outcome:** AI **delivers structured case studies**, improving **response relevance and depth**.

Best Practices for Iterative Prompt Refinement

- **Start Simple, Then Improve** – Begin with **basic prompts**, then **add details gradually**.
- **Analyze AI Weaknesses** – Identify **recurring issues** (ambiguity, lack of structure, excessive length).
- **Adjust Formatting** – Use **bullet points, numbered lists, or tables** for structured responses.
- **Limit Prompt Length When Necessary** – Overly complex prompts **may confuse AI**; simplify where needed.
- **Incorporate Role-Based Guidance** – Assign AI a **persona (e.g., "You are a digital marketing expert")** for better alignment.

Refining prompts **iteratively enhances AI-generated responses**, leading to **higher accuracy, clarity, and contextual relevance**. By applying **systematic adjustments**, AI outputs become **progressively more refined, reliable, and actionable** for diverse applications.

Fine-Tuning Prompts for Different AI Models

Different AI models, such as **ChatGPT, Bard, Claude, and LLaMA,** have unique training methodologies, parameter structures, and data processing mechanisms. As a result, a **single prompt** may yield **different responses** depending on the AI model used. **Fine-tuning prompts** for specific models is essential to **optimize accuracy, consistency, and usability** across various AI applications.

Why AI Models Respond Differently to the Same Prompt

AI models are trained on **diverse datasets** and have distinct architectures, which affect how they process and generate responses. Some factors influencing variations include:

1. **Training Data Sources** – Some models access **real-time web data (Google Bard)**, while others rely on **static datasets (ChatGPT-4, Claude)**.
2. **Token Processing Limits** – Different models handle **text length differently**, affecting **response depth and coherence**.
3. **Context Retention** – Some models **better maintain context in long conversations** than others.
4. **Parameter Scaling** – Larger models (GPT-4, Claude) tend to generate **more nuanced and context-aware responses** compared to smaller models (GPT-3.5, LLaMA).
5. **Bias and Tuning Preferences** – Models are fine-tuned with **different ethical, cultural, and response moderation policies**, affecting how they interpret prompts.

Adapting Prompts for Different AI Models

Since different AI models **respond uniquely**, prompts must be **fine-tuned** to align with each model's **capabilities and limitations**. Below are tailored strategies for refining prompts per model.

---

1. Optimizing Prompts for ChatGPT (OpenAI GPT-4, GPT-3.5)

Characteristics of ChatGPT

- **Strong reasoning and structured output generation**.
- **Limited real-time internet access** (as of the last model update).
- **Excellent for general knowledge, creative writing, and coding assistance**.
- **May generate verbose responses if not constrained**.

Prompt Fine-Tuning for ChatGPT

- **Explicitly state response constraints (word limit, format, tone)**.
- **Use role-based prompting for contextual accuracy**.
- **Avoid vague prompts—specify exact details needed**.

Example:

- **Weak Prompt:** "Explain how Bitcoin works."

- **Refined Prompt for ChatGPT:** "You are a cryptocurrency expert. Explain how Bitcoin transactions work, focusing on blockchain verification, proof-of-work mining, and security mechanisms in under 200 words."

2. Optimizing Prompts for Bard (Google AI)

Characteristics of Bard

- **Access to real-time internet data.**
- **Stronger at retrieving up-to-date news, trends, and recent research.**
- **Can sometimes be inconsistent in structured formatting.**

Prompt Fine-Tuning for Bard

- **Leverage its real-time search capability by requesting the latest data.**
- **Request specific sources or citations for better reliability.**
- **Use concise and structured prompts to reduce response drift.**

Example:

- **Weak Prompt:** "What are the current trends in AI?"
- **Refined Prompt for Bard:** "Retrieve and summarize three of the most recent advancements in artificial intelligence from 2024, including key players and breakthrough innovations. Provide citations where possible."

3. Optimizing Prompts for Claude (Anthropic AI)

Characteristics of Claude

- **Strong focus on ethical AI and bias reduction.**
- **Good for detailed explanations, analysis, and philosophy.**
- **Better than some models at handling complex multi-turn conversations.**

Prompt Fine-Tuning for Claude

- **Use prompts that require logical reasoning and ethical considerations.**
- **Encourage multi-turn interactions by referencing previous context.**
- **Avoid overly directive commands—let AI interpret topics naturally.**

Example:

- **Weak Prompt:** "List the pros and cons of AI in business."

- **Refined Prompt for Claude:** "Analyze the ethical and economic impact of AI in business. Include both short-term and long-term consequences from an economic and workforce perspective."

---

4. Optimizing Prompts for LLaMA (Meta AI)

Characteristics of LLaMA

- **Designed primarily for research and technical applications.**
- **More compact and efficient but requires well-structured prompts for optimal performance.**
- **Best suited for developers and AI researchers.**

Prompt Fine-Tuning for LLaMA

- **Use highly structured, direct prompts to optimize efficiency.**
- **Avoid overly creative prompts—LLaMA excels in technical and factual inquiries.**
- **Include precise terminologies for research and academic use.**

Example:

- **Weak Prompt:** "Explain deep learning."
- **Refined Prompt for LLaMA:** "Provide a detailed technical breakdown of deep learning architectures, including CNNs, RNNs, and transformers, with a focus on their applications in AI model training."

Table: Prompt Refinement Techniques and Their Impact

The following table outlines different **prompt refinement strategies** and their direct impact on AI responses across different models.

Refinement Technique	Description	Impact on AI Response

Adding Role-Based Context	Assigns AI a **specific identity** (e.g., expert, professor, lawyer) to improve response precision.	Ensures AI **stays on topic and provides domain-specific insights**.
Constraining Output Format	Specifies **structured responses** such as lists, paragraphs, or tables.	Reduces **ambiguity and increases readability**.
Providing Step-by-Step Instructions	Encourages AI to **explain complex topics in sequential logic**.	Produces **clearer, logically sound responses**.
Adjusting Prompt Length	Uses **concise but informative prompts** to avoid unnecessary details.	Prevents **verbose or overly simplistic answers**.
Incorporating Few-Shot Learning	Includes **examples within the prompt** to guide AI behavior.	Improves **accuracy and consistency in AI-generated content**.
Leveraging Multi-Turn Refinement	Iteratively refines prompts based on AI's **previous response**.	Enhances **AI adaptability and precision over multiple interactions**.
Defining Word Limits or Response Scope	Restricts AI's output length and scope **to avoid unnecessary information**.	Provides **concise, to-the-point responses without excessive details**.
Specifying Data Retrieval Requirements	Encourages AI to fetch **real-time data (for Bard) or avoid outdated information (for ChatGPT, Claude, LLaMA)**.	Ensures **accuracy in time-sensitive queries**.

Key Takeaways for Optimizing AI Prompts

1. **Each AI model responds differently to the same prompt.**

   - ChatGPT handles **structured queries and in-depth explanations well**.
   - Bard is better for **real-time data retrieval and factual updates**.
   - Claude excels in **logical, ethical, and long-form reasoning**.
   - LLaMA is optimized for **technical and research-based queries**.
2. **Fine-tuning prompts by incorporating constraints, structure, and role-based context significantly improves AI output quality.**

3. **Refining prompts iteratively based on AI's response behavior** is key to achieving more **accurate, structured, and contextually relevant outputs**.

By systematically refining prompts using these techniques, users can **maximize the effectiveness of AI interactions**, ensuring that responses are **precise, well-structured, and relevant to specific use cases**.

Chapter 8

Temperature, Tokens, and Model Parameters

Understanding AI Model Parameters and Their Effects

Introduction to AI Model Parameters

AI models, such as **ChatGPT, Claude, and LLaMA**, generate text by **predicting the most probable sequence of words** based on user prompts. Several key parameters control **how creative, deterministic, or constrained** these responses are. By adjusting these parameters, users can **fine-tune AI outputs** to meet different needs, from factual accuracy to creative storytelling.

The most commonly used AI model parameters include:

Parameter	Description	Effect on AI Responses
Temperature	Controls randomness in text generation.	Higher values (e.g., 1.0) make responses **more creative and unpredictable**; lower values (e.g., 0.2) make responses **more focused and deterministic**.
Top-P (Nucleus Sampling)	Filters out low-probability words.	A lower **Top-P** value narrows word choices, making responses **more controlled**. Higher values allow **wider word selection**.
Max Tokens	Limits response length.	Determines how many words/characters AI can generate in one response.
Top-K Sampling	Restricts word selection to the **K most likely words**.	Lower values create **more structured responses**, while higher values **increase randomness**.

Frequency Penalty	Penalizes frequent word repetition.	Helps **reduce redundancy** in AI responses.
Presence Penalty	Encourages introduction of new words/concepts.	Increases **topic diversity** in responses.

Understanding these parameters allows users to **fine-tune AI behavior**, optimizing outputs for specific tasks such as **formal writing, coding, storytelling, or conversational AI**.

How Temperature and Top-P Influence Randomness

Temperature: Controlling AI Creativity

Temperature **adjusts the level of randomness** in AI responses, affecting how predictable or diverse the text will be.

- **Low Temperature (0.1 - 0.3):** AI chooses the **most probable words**, creating highly **structured, factual, and repetitive responses**.
- **Medium Temperature (0.4 - 0.7):** AI balances **coherence and creativity**, making responses more **varied yet reliable**.
- **High Temperature (0.8 - 1.5):** AI chooses **less predictable words**, making responses **more creative, open-ended, and diverse**.

Examples of Temperature in AI Output

Prompt:

"Describe a sunset over the ocean."

Temperature	AI Response Example
0.2	"The sun sets, casting an orange glow over the calm ocean waves. The sky darkens as stars begin to appear."
0.7	"The sun melts into the horizon, blending shades of tangerine and violet as waves shimmer with golden reflections."
1.2	"A fiery orb descends, spilling molten gold across rippling tides, while deep indigo swirls chase the vanishing light."

A **low temperature** setting provides a **straightforward and structured** response, while a **high temperature** setting allows **more poetic and imaginative** output.

Top-P (Nucleus Sampling): Filtering Word Choices

Top-P (or nucleus sampling) adjusts how the AI selects words by **limiting the probability range** from which the model chooses its next word.

- **Lower Top-P values (e.g., 0.1 - 0.3):** AI **chooses from a very small set** of highly probable words, making responses **more controlled and deterministic**.
- **Higher Top-P values (e.g., 0.7 - 1.0):** AI **considers a broader set of possible words**, increasing **variation and creativity** in responses.

Examples of Top-P in AI Output

Prompt:

"Tell a short futuristic story about space travel."

Top-P Value	AI Response Example
0.2	"In 2054, astronauts landed on Mars using nuclear propulsion. They established a research base and began terraforming."
0.7	"By 2070, humanity ventured beyond Mars, colonizing Europa's icy surface, where researchers uncovered signs of microbial life."
1.0	"The year is 2099, and a quantum-accelerated spacecraft, piloted by an AI consciousness, glides through a wormhole toward a distant galaxy."

With a **low Top-P setting**, the AI sticks to **high-probability words**, resulting in **factual and predictable storytelling**. Higher values introduce **more creativity, variation, and unexpected elements**.

When to Adjust Temperature vs. Top-P

Scenario	Best Setting	Why?

Academic Writing	Temperature: 0.2 - 0.3, Top-P: 0.2 - 0.5	Ensures factual accuracy and structured responses.
Creative Writing (Fiction, Poetry, etc.)	Temperature: 0.8 - 1.2, Top-P: 0.7 - 1.0	Encourages imaginative, unpredictable storytelling.
Programming Assistance	Temperature: 0.1 - 0.3, Top-P: 0.2 - 0.4	Ensures consistent, logical code output.
Marketing & Ad Copy	Temperature: 0.5 - 0.8, Top-P: 0.5 - 0.9	Generates persuasive yet structured content.
Casual Conversations	Temperature: 0.6 - 1.0, Top-P: 0.7 - 1.0	Makes AI responses sound more natural and engaging.

By adjusting **temperature and Top-P together**, users can fine-tune AI behavior to align with their specific needs, whether it's producing **formal, structured responses or highly creative and imaginative text**.

Key Takeaways for Model Parameters

- **Temperature controls randomness**, affecting whether responses are more predictable or creative.
- **Top-P narrows or expands word selection**, influencing how structured or diverse responses are.

- Lower values of Temperature and Top-P create more factual, precise, and controlled outputs.
- Higher values make responses more open-ended, unpredictable, and imaginative.
- Understanding how these parameters interact allows for fine-tuned AI prompting across different applications.

By mastering **AI model parameters**, users can optimize **response quality, creativity, and accuracy**—enhancing both **practical applications and creative exploration** with AI.

Managing Token Limits for Longer Conversations

Understanding Token Limits in AI Models

Artificial Intelligence (AI) models process text using **tokens**, which are units of words, subwords, or characters. Every AI model has a **token limit**, which defines how much text the model can process in a single request or conversation. Managing token limits is crucial for ensuring AI provides **coherent, contextual, and relevant responses, especially in long-form interactions**.

Why Token Limits Matter

1. **Prevents Truncation of Responses**

   - If a conversation exceeds the model's token capacity, AI may **truncate or forget previous parts** of the interaction.
   - Example: In a 4,096-token model, if the conversation exceeds the limit, earlier messages may be discarded.
2. **Maintains Context in Long Conversations**

   - AI models **lose memory of earlier interactions** once they surpass the token window, making it harder to sustain detailed discussions.
3. **Optimizes Computational Efficiency**

   - AI models with large token requirements **consume more computational power**, affecting performance and cost for API-based interactions.

4. **Prevents Loss of Key Information**

    o   Token overflow **removes earlier details**, potentially leading AI to **repeat questions, misunderstand instructions, or generate redundant responses**.

Token Limits Across Popular AI Models

AI Model	Token Limit	Usage Notes
GPT-4 Turbo	~128,000 tokens	Best for long conversations and document-level analysis.
GPT-4	8,192 tokens	Handles moderate-length discussions but loses context over extended dialogue.
GPT-3.5	4,096 tokens	Requires careful token management in longer conversations.
Google Bard	Not publicly disclosed	Can reference past responses but may drift off-topic in extended interactions.
Claude (Anthropic AI)	100,000 tokens	Strong context retention, suitable for in-depth discussions.
LLaMA 2 (Meta AI)	4,096 - 32,000 tokens	Good for research but limited in conversational memory.

Managing token limits ensures AI-generated responses remain **coherent, structured, and contextually aware**, even in **lengthy interactions**.

Strategies for Managing Token Limits in AI Conversations

To optimize responses in longer conversations, **users must structure their prompts and interactions effectively**. Below are key techniques:

1. Use Summarization to Retain Context

When engaging in long-form interactions, **request periodic summaries** to maintain conversation flow.

- **Example Without Summarization:**

    - User: "Can you explain neural networks?"
    - AI: **Explains neural networks in detail**.
    - User: "Now tell me how they relate to deep learning."
    - AI: **Repeats some earlier details instead of focusing on deep learning.**
- **Example With Summarization:**

    - User: "Summarize our discussion so far in 100 words before explaining how neural networks relate to deep learning."
    - AI: **Generates a concise summary, retaining key points.**

By actively **summarizing key points**, AI retains the **core conversation context within token limits**.

---

2. Split Long Queries into Modular Sections

Instead of overwhelming AI with **one large, detailed question**, break it into **smaller, focused queries**.

- **Ineffective Prompt:**

    - "Explain blockchain technology, its applications in finance, healthcare, and supply chain, and compare proof-of-work vs. proof-of-stake consensus mechanisms."
- **Optimized Modular Prompts:**

    - "First, explain blockchain technology in simple terms."

- "Now, describe blockchain applications in finance, healthcare, and supply chain."
- "Finally, compare proof-of-work and proof-of-stake consensus mechanisms."

This approach **ensures clarity, reduces token overload, and improves response coherence**.

---

3. Set Response Constraints to Reduce Token Consumption

AI responses can be **verbose** by default. Defining constraints **controls response length and prevents excessive token usage**.

- **Example Without Constraints:**

  - "Explain the history of the internet."
  - AI: **Generates an excessively long response spanning multiple decades.**
- **Example With Constraints:**

  - "Explain the history of the internet in 200 words, focusing on key milestones like ARPANET, the World Wide Web, and broadband development."

By setting word limits, users **ensure concise responses** while **saving tokens for follow-up queries**.

---

4. Utilize Role-Based Summaries for Efficiency

Instead of repeating details, AI can **summarize its previous response in a structured format**.

- **Example Without Optimization:**

  - User: "Explain quantum computing."
  - AI: **Provides an in-depth explanation.**
  - User: "Can you summarize that?"
  - AI: **Repeats unnecessary details, consuming tokens.**

- **Optimized Role-Based Summary Prompt:**

  - "Summarize your explanation of quantum computing as if you're teaching it to a high school student, using simple terms."

This **reduces token usage while ensuring clarity**.

---

5. Periodically Reset the Conversation for Context Retention

When token limits are reached, **resetting AI's context can prevent loss of earlier discussion points**.

- **Example Without Reset:**

  - AI loses track of previous messages and **begins repeating earlier points**.
- **Example With Reset:**

  - "Let's start fresh: summarize what we've discussed so far in a structured format, and I'll ask my next question based on that summary."

By **restarting the conversation strategically**, users **prevent AI from losing track of important context**.

Illustration: Adjusting Model Parameters for Optimal Results

To visually demonstrate **how adjusting AI model parameters impacts responses**, the following flowchart outlines key **prompt refinement and token management techniques**:

plaintext
CopyEdit

```
+------------------------------------------------+
|  User Inputs Initial Prompt                    |
+------------------------------------------------+
```

```
                                 |
                                 v
        +--------------------------------------------------------+
        |   AI Generates Response                                |
        |   (Checks token usage and response length)             |
        +--------------------------------------------------------+

                                 |
        |   Does AI exceed token limit?                          |
        |      (Yes)                  |          (No)            |
        |                             |                          |
        v                             v                          v
+------------------------------+   +------------------------------+
+------------------------------+
|  Truncate Excess Tokens      |   |  Maintain Conversation       |
|  Reduce Response Length      |
|  Summarize Key Details       |   |  Continue Prompt Sequence    |
|  Request Shortened Output    |
+------------------------------+   +------------------------------+
+------------------------------+

                                 |
                                 v
                +----------------------------------------------+
                |   User Adjusts Prompt for Optimization       |
                |   (Modular Sections, Constraints Applied)    |
                +----------------------------------------------+

                                 |
                                 v
                +----------------------------------------------+
                |   AI Generates More Efficient Response       |
                |   (Token Management Optimized)               |
                +----------------------------------------------+
```

This **flowchart highlights the importance of prompt refinement** and token control for **optimal AI response generation**.

Key Takeaways for Managing Token Limits

1. **Token limits affect response quality** – exceeding them may cause AI to **lose earlier context**.

2. **Summarization preserves key information** – instruct AI to **generate concise summaries** when nearing token capacity.

3. **Breaking queries into modular sections improves clarity** – structured prompts yield **better responses with less token consumption**.

4. **Using response constraints optimizes output length** – specifying word limits prevents **excessive verbosity**.

5. **Resetting conversations strategically prevents context loss** – periodically **restarting discussions** maintains **logical flow**.

By managing token limits effectively, users can **enhance AI-generated responses, maintain conversational continuity, and optimize computational efficiency** in longer interactions.

Chapter 9

Multi-Turn Conversational Prompting

Designing Prompts for Context-Rich Conversations

What is Multi-Turn Conversational Prompting?

Multi-turn conversational prompting refers to the **continuous interaction between AI and users** across multiple exchanges, where AI maintains **context, coherence, and consistency** over time. Unlike single-turn prompting, where each request is independent, multi-turn interactions **simulate natural dialogue**, ensuring AI **remembers prior responses and builds upon them**.

Why Multi-Turn Prompting is Essential?

- **Maintains Context** – AI retains information from previous messages, allowing for more **meaningful and relevant responses**.
- **Enhances Logical Flow** – Ensures AI **builds on prior exchanges**, creating **progressive, structured discussions**.
- **Supports Complex Conversations** – Useful for **technical support, education, and business negotiations**, where details need to be carried forward.
- **Improves Personalization** – AI adapts based on previous interactions, mimicking **human-like continuity** in dialogue.

Challenges in Multi-Turn Prompting

1. **Context Loss Due to Token Limits** – AI models have a **finite token window**, meaning earlier exchanges may be forgotten.
2. **Drift in AI Responses** – AI may **contradict earlier responses** if the conversation becomes too lengthy.
3. **Lack of Precision in Context Recall** – AI might **misinterpret prior details**, leading to inconsistencies.
4. **Unnecessary Repetitions** – AI may **reiterate previously provided details**, leading to inefficiency.

Techniques for Designing Context-Rich Prompts

1. Using Role-Based Prompting for Consistency

Defining AI's role at the start **ensures consistent behavior throughout the conversation**.

- **Example Without Role Assignment:**

    - User: "Explain blockchain."
    - AI: "Blockchain is a decentralized technology…"
    - User: "Now explain how it applies to banking."
    - AI: *Response may lack depth due to no defined role.*
- **Optimized Role-Based Prompt:**

    - User: "You are a fintech expert. Explain blockchain technology."
    - AI: "As a fintech expert, I can tell you that blockchain is…"
    - User: "Now explain how it applies to banking."
    - AI: *Response stays within the fintech context, ensuring coherence.*

2. Structuring Initial Prompts for Long Conversations

- **Clearly define AI's task upfront** to ensure consistency across exchanges.

- **State the topic scope** to **avoid unnecessary topic shifts**.

- **Example:**

    - **Weak Prompt:** "Tell me about Python programming."
    - **Refined Multi-Turn Prompt:**
        - "We will have a step-by-step discussion about Python programming. In this conversation:
            1. You will start by explaining Python's history and use cases.
            2. Next, I will ask about data structures and control flow.
            3. Then, we will discuss object-oriented programming. Let's begin: Explain Python's history and its primary use cases."

By **framing the conversation as a structured discussion**, AI follows a **logical flow** rather than producing scattered responses.

3. Summarizing Previous Responses to Retain Context

84

To **prevent AI from losing context**, periodically request **summaries of previous interactions** before proceeding.

- **Example:**
  - User: "Summarize what we've discussed about Python's history before moving on to data structures."
  - AI: *Generates a brief recap, ensuring key details are retained for the next segment.*

This technique **optimizes token usage** and **improves AI's ability to recall past exchanges**.

4. Using Reference Tokens to Anchor Conversations

- Instead of assuming AI **remembers prior responses**, explicitly **reference previous statements**.

- **Example Without Reference Tokens:**

  - User: "Tell me about quantum computing."
  - AI: *Explains quantum computing basics.*
  - User: "How does it apply to cryptography?"
  - AI: *Might not fully connect the concepts.*
- **Example With Reference Tokens:**

  - User: "Based on your previous explanation of quantum computing, describe its impact on cryptography."
  - AI: *Acknowledges previous discussion, ensuring seamless continuity.*

This **reinforces continuity and avoids contradictions**.

5. Establishing Boundaries to Prevent AI Drift

AI can sometimes **veer off-topic** over extended conversations. Setting clear **topic boundaries** ensures it **remains focused**.

- **Example Without Boundaries:**

  - User: "Tell me about cloud computing."
  - AI: *Explains cloud computing basics.*
  - User: "And how does blockchain fit into this?"
  - AI: *Shifts into blockchain without maintaining relevance to cloud computing.*

- **Example With Defined Boundaries:**

  - User: "Explain cloud computing. Focus only on SaaS, PaaS, and IaaS without discussing blockchain."
  - AI: *Provides a precise, scoped response, avoiding unrelated topics.*

Boundaries **prevent AI from diverging too far** from the intended subject matter.

Keeping AI Responses Consistent Across Multiple Interactions

Why Consistency is Crucial in Multi-Turn Conversations

Inconsistent AI responses **reduce credibility** and **create confusion**, especially in **technical, business, or academic discussions**. Ensuring **uniformity in responses** makes AI more **reliable and professional**.

Challenges in Maintaining AI Response Consistency

1. **Forgetting Past Information** – Due to **token constraints**, AI may **lose earlier context**.
2. **Contradicting Earlier Statements** – AI may **change its stance** if not explicitly guided.
3. **Variability in Explanation Styles** – AI may switch between **technical and simplified explanations** inconsistently.

Techniques for Keeping AI Responses Consistent

1. Reinforcing Memory with Context Recap

- **Periodically reintroduce key details** from earlier exchanges to **anchor AI's memory**.
- **Example:**
  - User: "Previously, you mentioned cloud computing benefits. Summarize them before we move forward."
  - AI: *Reinforces previous discussion, ensuring coherence.*

2. Using Persistent Role-Based Prompting

- Assign AI a **fixed role** across multiple turns to prevent inconsistencies.

- **Example Without Role Consistency:**

  - User: "Explain blockchain for beginners."
  - AI: *Provides a simplified explanation.*
  - User: "Now, explain blockchain for financial institutions."
  - AI: *Response may lack depth due to a shift in audience focus.*
- **Optimized Prompt for Consistency:**

  - User: "You are a blockchain analyst. Explain blockchain for beginners."
  - AI: *Provides a beginner-friendly explanation within financial contexts.*
  - User: "Now, provide a more technical explanation for financial institutions."
  - AI: *Maintains its role, ensuring depth and accuracy.*

3. Structuring Follow-Up Prompts for Coherence

- Instead of allowing **open-ended follow-ups**, ensure **structured progression**.

- **Example Without Structured Follow-Ups:**

  - User: "What are the benefits of AI?"
  - AI: *Lists benefits.*
  - User: "Tell me about its risks."
  - AI: *May not connect risks to benefits properly.*
- **Example With Structured Progression:**

  - User: "You listed AI benefits earlier. Now, explain risks associated with those specific benefits."
  - AI: *Provides a well-connected response, ensuring logical continuity.*

4. Preventing Repetitive or Contradictory Responses

- If AI **begins repeating information**, refine prompts to **eliminate redundancy**.
- **Example:**
  - User: "Provide additional details without repeating what you mentioned earlier."

This **ensures AI introduces new insights** rather than reiterating old content.

Key Takeaways for Multi-Turn Prompting

1. **Context-rich prompts guide AI through extended discussions** – Defining **role, scope, and sequence** improves logical flow.

2. **Using reference tokens and structured prompts prevents AI drift** – Reinforcing past discussions helps **retain consistency**.

3. **Summarization techniques improve long-form interactions** – Asking AI to **recap key points before moving forward** enhances continuity.

4. **Boundaries prevent AI from going off-topic** – Setting **explicit focus areas** ensures **response relevance**.

5. **Persistent role-based prompting ensures AI consistency** – Assigning AI a **clear identity throughout interactions** leads to **uniform explanations**.

By implementing **structured multi-turn prompting**, users can create **engaging, contextually aware, and logically consistent AI conversations**, optimizing **AI's ability to function as a reliable dialogue partner**.

Best Practices for Long-Term Memory in AI Conversations

Understanding Long-Term Memory in AI Conversations

AI models, particularly **large language models (LLMs) like ChatGPT, Bard, Claude, and LLaMA**, process conversations in chunks using **token windows**. While they can remember **previous exchanges within a session**, they do not have **persistent long-term memory** unless explicitly designed with **memory storage and retrieval mechanisms** (e.g., fine-tuned models with vector databases).

For applications requiring **ongoing context retention over extended interactions**, users must **actively manage how AI maintains and recalls past conversations** to avoid **information loss, contradictions, and inconsistencies**.

Challenges in Maintaining Long-Term AI Memory

1. **Token Window Limitations**

   - AI **forgets earlier parts of a conversation** once its token limit is exceeded.
   - Models with larger token limits (e.g., **Claude with 100K tokens**) perform better in retaining extended discussions.
2. **Loss of Historical Context**

   - If an AI **cannot reference prior interactions**, it may **contradict itself or repeat prior statements**.
3. **Inconsistent Tone or Focus**

   - Over extended conversations, AI may **drift from the original topic** or **change response style**.
4. **Redundant Information Repetition**

   - AI may **restate previous details unnecessarily**, wasting token capacity.

Best Practices for Maintaining Context in Multi-Turn AI Conversations

To **extend AI's effective memory**, users must **optimize prompts, summarize discussions, and manage context references efficiently**.

1. Use Explicit Context Carry-Over Techniques

Instead of assuming AI **remembers all previous interactions**, users should **explicitly reintroduce key details** in new prompts.

- **Example Without Context Carry-Over:**

    - User: *"Tell me about renewable energy."*
    - AI: *Gives a basic definition.*
    - User (5 messages later): *"Explain its impact on the economy."*
    - AI: *Might not connect the economic impact to previous discussions.*
- **Example With Context Carry-Over:**

    - User: *"Previously, you explained renewable energy. Now, connect it to its impact on the economy."*
    - AI: *Acknowledges earlier points and builds upon them logically.*

---

2. Use Summaries to Reinforce AI's Memory

Summarizing key details at regular intervals **helps AI recall past exchanges within token limits**.

- **Example of a Prompt Requesting a Summary:**
    - *"Summarize our discussion so far in 100 words before we continue with the next topic."*

This ensures **important details remain within the token window** while reducing **irrelevant repetition**.

---

3. Assign AI a Persistent Role to Maintain Consistency

Defining AI's role in the **beginning of a conversation** ensures it **retains a consistent tone, knowledge depth, and domain focus**.

- **Example:**
    - *"For this conversation, you are a cybersecurity expert. Provide all responses from that perspective."*

When AI drifts, users can **reinforce the role** by saying:

- *"Reaffirming that you are speaking as a cybersecurity expert, please continue…"*

This **prevents shifts in explanation styles** and **ensures expertise consistency**.

4. Break Down Conversations into Modular Segments

Instead of asking for a **broad, multi-topic response at once**, divide the discussion into **smaller, structured segments**.

- **Example Without Modular Segments:**

    1. *"Explain artificial intelligence, its history, applications, risks, and ethical concerns."*
- **Optimized Modular Approach:**

    1. *"First, explain the history of artificial intelligence."*
    2. *"Now, describe AI's modern applications in healthcare and finance."*
    3. *"Next, outline the risks associated with AI adoption."*
    4. *"Finally, discuss AI ethics, including bias and accountability."*

This **prevents information overload**, **ensures logical flow**, and **improves AI response quality**.

5. Use Context Anchors to Prevent Contradictions

If AI begins contradicting earlier statements, **explicitly anchor responses to prior information**.

- **Example Without Context Anchoring:**

    - User (earlier in conversation): *"Explain the causes of climate change."*
    - AI: *Lists greenhouse gases, deforestation, etc.*
    - User (later): *"Is deforestation a major cause of climate change?"*
    - AI: *Might contradict its earlier answer if it does not recall the context.*
- **Example With Context Anchoring:**

    - User: *"Based on your previous explanation of climate change causes, expand on deforestation's role."*
    - AI: *Recognizes the reference and provides a detailed, consistent follow-up.*

This technique **minimizes inconsistencies** in AI-generated responses.

6. Periodically Reset the Conversation with Key Context Points

If the conversation **becomes too long**, AI may **lose critical early details**. Reset the discussion by **restating core points concisely**.

- **Example Resetting Context Mid-Conversation:**
  - *"To ensure we stay on track, here's a summary of what we've covered: [Insert Key Points]. Now, let's move on to the next topic."*

This **prevents AI from losing important details due to token window constraints**.

Flowchart: Managing Context in Multi-Turn Conversations

The following flowchart outlines **an optimized approach to managing AI memory in extended interactions**.

plaintext
CopyEdit

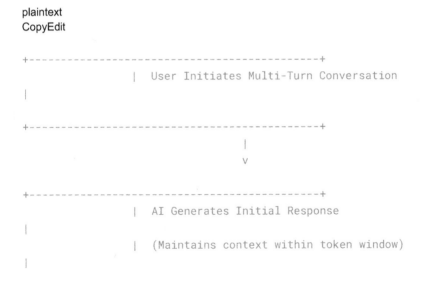

```
+----------------------------------------------+
                  |  User Initiates Multi-Turn Conversation
  |
+----------------------------------------------+
                                |
                                v
+----------------------------------------------+
                  |  AI Generates Initial Response
  |
                  |  (Maintains context within token window)
  |
```

```
+----------------------------------------------+
                                |
                |  Is the conversation exceeding token limit?
|
                |        (Yes)                 |           (No)
|
                |                              |
|
                v                              v
v
    +----------------------------+
+----------------------------+  +----------------------------+
  | Request Summary to Retain |  | Continue Normal Exchange
|  | Reinforce Prior Details  |
  | Key Discussion Points     |  | AI retains context
|  | Using Reference Prompts   |
    +----------------------------+
+----------------------------+  +----------------------------+
                                |
                                v

+------------------------------------------------+
                |  User Reintroduces Context When Needed
|
                |  (Reference earlier discussion)
|
+------------------------------------------------+
                |
                v

+------------------------------------------------+
                |  AI Generates Coherent Response
|
                |  (Minimizes Contradictions & Redundancy)
|
```

```
  +---------------------------------------------+
                                              |
                                              v
  +---------------------------------------------+
                  |  User Periodically Resets Discussion
  |
                  |  (Summarizes Key Topics to Reinforce AI)
  |
  +---------------------------------------------+
                                              |
                                              v
  +---------------------------------------------+
                  |  Multi-Turn Conversation Remains Effective
  |
                  |  (Maintains Logical Flow and Accuracy)
  |
  +---------------------------------------------+
```

This structured **memory management approach** ensures AI **remains contextually aware, reduces inconsistencies, and sustains logical, coherent responses**.

Key Takeaways for Managing AI Memory in Multi-Turn Conversations

1. **Explicitly reference prior interactions** – Do not assume AI **remembers every detail**; reintroduce key points when necessary.

2. **Use summarization techniques** – Periodically **request AI to summarize prior discussions** to retain core details within token limits.

3. **Assign AI a consistent role** – Defining AI's role from the start **ensures expertise and tone uniformity**.

4. **Break complex discussions into modular parts** – Instead of **overloading AI with broad topics**, structure conversations **step by step**.

5. **Use context anchoring to prevent contradictions** – Explicitly **link new prompts to earlier responses** for continuity.

6. **Periodically reset the conversation with concise summaries** – This **prevents AI from losing critical information due to token constraints**.

By applying these **best practices**, users can optimize AI conversations for **long-term consistency, logical flow, and improved contextual awareness**, ensuring **reliable and meaningful AI-assisted interactions**.

Chapter 10

AI Prompting for Content Creation

Writing Blogs, Articles, and Creative Stories with AI

Introduction to AI in Content Creation

Content creation is one of the most popular applications of AI, enabling writers, marketers, and businesses to **generate high-quality text efficiently**. AI models like **ChatGPT, Bard, Claude, and LLaMA** can assist with writing **blogs, articles, creative stories, and marketing copy** by offering structured, engaging, and informative content.

However, achieving **human-like, high-quality writing** requires **well-designed prompts** to guide AI responses toward **clarity, coherence, and engagement**. The right prompts ensure AI-generated content is **factually accurate, structured, and free from redundancy**.

Writing Blogs and Articles with AI

1. Importance of Well-Structured AI Prompts in Article Writing

While AI can generate content instantly, poorly designed prompts can lead to **generic, unstructured, or irrelevant outputs**. A **strong prompt** for article writing should include:

- **A clear topic definition** (e.g., "Write about sustainable energy practices.")
- **A specified tone and audience** (e.g., "Write in a professional tone for business executives.")
- **A structured format** (e.g., "Provide an introduction, three key sections, and a conclusion.")
- **Factual accuracy requests** (e.g., "Include data-driven insights with citations where possible.")

2. Example Prompts for Blog and Article Writing

General Blog Post Prompt

"Write a 1,500-word blog post about the benefits of mindfulness in daily life. Structure the content into an introduction, key benefits (mental health, productivity, relationships), and a conclusion. Maintain an engaging yet informative tone, and provide practical examples."

SEO-Optimized Article Prompt

"Write an SEO-friendly 2,000-word article on 'The Future of Electric Vehicles.' Include keyword optimization, use subheadings, bullet points, and data-backed insights. Target a tech-savvy audience with a formal yet engaging tone."

Technical Blog Post Prompt

"Write a technical blog post explaining blockchain technology to non-technical readers. Use simple analogies, structured headings, and clear explanations. Avoid excessive jargon and focus on real-world applications."

Industry-Specific Article Prompt

"Write an article for healthcare professionals about how artificial intelligence is transforming medical diagnostics. Include case studies, statistical data, and expert opinions where applicable."

3. Enhancing Blog Engagement with AI

To make AI-generated blogs more **engaging and reader-friendly**, prompts should include:

Conversational or storytelling elements – "Start with a short personal anecdote about overcoming stress through meditation."

Use of examples and case studies – "Provide real-world examples of companies successfully using AI in marketing."

Data and statistics – "Include at least three statistics from credible sources."

Call-to-action (CTA) – "End with a compelling CTA encouraging readers to adopt AI tools for productivity."

Creative Story Writing with AI

1. AI's Role in Fiction Writing

AI can assist in writing **short stories, novels, screenplays, and poetry**. However, creative storytelling requires **imaginative elements, strong character development, and narrative depth**, which means **effective prompting** is essential to produce compelling results.

2. Structuring AI Prompts for Creative Writing

Character-Driven Story Prompt

"Write a short story about a detective investigating a mysterious disappearance in a small town. The protagonist is a former journalist with a troubled past. Include strong dialogue, suspenseful pacing, and an unexpected twist."

Genre-Specific Story Prompt

"Write a 2,000-word fantasy story about a young warrior who must retrieve an enchanted relic to save their kingdom. Include world-building details, character development, and an epic battle scene."

First-Person Narrative Prompt

"Write a dystopian sci-fi story in the first person. The protagonist is a scientist who discovers a secret government experiment. The tone should be suspenseful and introspective."

3. Enhancing AI-Generated Stories

To refine AI-generated stories, prompts should encourage:
   Character depth – "Describe the protagonist's internal conflict and motivations."
   Descriptive world-building – "Paint a vivid picture of the story's setting using sensory details."
   Plot twists and suspense – "Add an unexpected revelation at the climax."
   Dialogue-driven storytelling – "Use realistic and engaging character dialogue."

Structuring Prompts for Engaging and Readable Content

1. The Importance of Well-Structured Prompts

The way prompts are designed influences **the quality, readability, and engagement level** of AI-generated content. Well-structured prompts lead to **cohesive, logical, and audience-targeted content**.

2. Components of a Strong Writing Prompt

Component	Description	Example
Topic Definition	Clearly define the subject of the content.	"Write an article on the impact of AI on the job market."
Tone & Audience	Specify the desired writing tone and reader demographic.	"Use a professional tone for business executives."
Content Structure	Outline sections, subheadings, or format preferences.	"Organize into an introduction, three main points, and a conclusion."
Length Expectation	Specify word count to maintain readability.	"Write a 1,500-word blog post."
Engagement Techniques	Encourage storytelling, examples, or questions to captivate readers.	"Start with a real-world case study."

3. Examples of Well-Structured Content Prompts

Blog Post Prompt with Defined Structure

*"Write a 1,200-word blog post on 'How Remote Work is Changing the Workplace.'
99

- Introduction: Discuss the rise of remote work.
- Section 1: Benefits for employees (flexibility, productivity, work-life balance).
- Section 2: Challenges for companies (communication, collaboration, cybersecurity risks).
- Section 3: The future of remote work (predictions, technology, hybrid models).
- Conclusion: Summarize key points and offer actionable advice for companies adapting to remote work."*

News Article Prompt

"Write a 750-word news article on the latest trends in renewable energy. Include expert insights, government policies, and technological advancements. Maintain a neutral journalistic tone and cite sources where applicable."

Marketing Copy Prompt

"Write a compelling product description for a new smart fitness tracker. Highlight key features such as heart rate monitoring, sleep tracking, and mobile connectivity. Use persuasive language to appeal to health-conscious consumers."

---

4. Using AI for Editing and Enhancing Content

AI can also assist in **refining and improving existing content** by:

- **Rewriting for clarity** – "Rewrite this paragraph to make it clearer and more engaging."
- **Grammar and tone correction** – "Adjust this blog post to use a more conversational tone."
- **Expanding ideas** – "Provide additional details on the benefits of AI in education."
- **Summarization** – "Summarize this article into three key takeaways."

Key Takeaways for AI-Assisted Content Creation

1. **Well-structured prompts lead to high-quality AI-generated content.**

2. **Defining topic, tone, format, and audience ensures clarity and engagement.**
3. **AI can assist in both content generation and refinement, improving efficiency.**
4. **For storytelling, prompts should focus on character development, plot depth, and world-building.**
5. **SEO and marketing content benefit from structured, keyword-optimized AI prompts.**

By mastering **structured AI prompting**, writers and businesses can leverage AI to create **compelling, engaging, and well-organized content** that meets professional standards.

Optimizing AI for Social Media and Marketing Copy

The Role of AI in Social Media and Marketing Content

Social media and digital marketing require **concise, engaging, and high-impact content** to capture audience attention quickly. AI can assist in crafting **highly optimized posts, advertisements, email marketing content, and branding materials** with efficiency and creativity.

However, **generic AI-generated marketing copy often lacks brand identity, emotional appeal, and personalization**. By using **precisely structured prompts**, AI can generate **persuasive, brand-aligned, and audience-targeted content**.

---

1. AI for Social Media Content

Key Factors in AI-Generated Social Media Copy

- **Conciseness** – Posts should be **short, clear, and attention-grabbing**.
- **Engagement** – Content should **invite interaction (likes, shares, comments, or click-throughs)**.
- **Brand Voice** – AI-generated text must reflect **consistent brand personality**.

101

- **Trending and SEO Optimization** – AI should include **relevant hashtags, keywords, and trends**.

---

2. Social Media Prompting Examples

Twitter (X) Post Prompt

"Write a viral Twitter post about the benefits of intermittent fasting. Keep it under 280 characters, use an engaging hook, and include two relevant hashtags."

Instagram Caption Prompt

"Create an Instagram caption for a luxury travel agency promoting a vacation package to the Maldives. Use a poetic, aspirational tone, include emojis, and add a call-to-action encouraging bookings."

LinkedIn Thought Leadership Prompt

"Write a LinkedIn post for a tech CEO discussing the impact of AI on job automation. Maintain a professional tone, include industry insights, and encourage audience discussion."

Facebook Ad Copy Prompt

"Write a high-converting Facebook ad promoting a new smart home security system. Highlight safety benefits, create urgency, and include a compelling call-to-action directing users to a landing page."

---

3. AI for Marketing Copywriting

Key Elements of Effective AI-Generated Marketing Copy

Emotional appeal – AI should tap into **audience pain points and desires**.
Persuasive language – AI-generated copy must include **strong, action-driven wording**.

Storytelling techniques – Use narratives to create **connection and engagement**.
Brand alignment – AI copy must reflect the **company's unique voice and values**.

4. Marketing Copy Prompting Examples

Email Marketing Subject Line Prompt

"Generate five high-converting email subject lines for a Black Friday sale on electronics. Use urgency and personalization."

Product Description Prompt

"Write a product description for a new wireless noise-canceling headphone. Focus on premium audio quality, comfort, and long battery life. Keep the tone luxurious and persuasive."

Landing Page Headline Prompt

"Create a compelling landing page headline for an online course on digital marketing. Make it persuasive and emphasize career growth potential."

E-Commerce Ad Copy Prompt

"Write a short, persuasive Google Ad copy for a limited-time sale on organic skincare products. Include keywords like 'natural beauty,' 'eco-friendly,' and 'shop now.'"

5. Crafting AI-Optimized Call-to-Actions (CTAs)

A **Call-to-Action (CTA)** is crucial for **driving conversions** in social media posts, emails, ads, and websites.

Examples of AI-Optimized CTAs

For Sales: "Shop now and get 20% off – limited time only!"
For Newsletter Signups: "Subscribe today and receive exclusive industry insights."
For Event Registrations: "Reserve your seat for the AI Summit – spots are filling fast!"
For Engagement: "Tell us in the comments: What's your go-to productivity hack?"

Using **AI for CTA optimization** ensures copy **guides users toward action effectively**.

---

6. AI-Driven Personalization for Marketing Copy

Modern AI tools enable **hyper-personalization** in marketing copy, tailoring messages to **individual user preferences, behavior, and demographics**.

- **Example of Personalized Email Subject Line Prompt:**
  - *"Generate five personalized email subject lines for an abandoned cart reminder, using the customer's first name and the product they left in their cart."*

By **leveraging AI-driven personalization**, brands can significantly **increase engagement, open rates, and conversions**.

Table: Best Practices for AI-Generated Content

Best Practice	Description	Example Application
Define the Audience	Ensure AI knows the target **age, interests, and demographics**.	"Write an Instagram post targeting Gen Z fashion lovers."
Specify Tone & Style	AI should follow a **brand-aligned voice** (formal, playful, persuasive).	"Create an email campaign in a friendly, conversational tone."
Set Content Length	AI-generated content should meet **platform-specific character limits**.	"Write a Twitter post under 280 characters."
Use Strong CTAs	AI should include **action-driven wording** to boost conversions.	"End with a CTA that encourages sign-ups for a webinar."

Incorporate Keywords & SEO	AI must integrate **relevant keywords** for search optimization.	"Generate an SEO-friendly blog post on fitness nutrition."
Include Personalization	AI copy should feel **tailored** to individuals.	"Create a personalized ad for a returning customer on an e-commerce site."
Optimize for Mobile	AI should generate **concise, scannable content for mobile users**.	"Write an email that is mobile-friendly and under 200 words."
Test & Iterate	AI-generated copy should be **A/B tested** for performance.	"Generate two variations of a social media ad to test engagement."

7. Key Takeaways for AI-Powered Marketing & Social Media Copy

AI-generated content should be audience-specific, engaging, and concise.
 Marketing copy must include persuasive language, strong CTAs, and emotional appeal.
 Social media content should be optimized for virality, interaction, and SEO.
 AI personalization improves engagement, making messages feel human and tailored.
 Testing AI-generated content ensures high-performance results.

By applying **structured AI prompting techniques**, marketers can create **highly effective, conversion-driven content** that resonates with audiences across **multiple platforms**.

Chapter 11

AI Prompting for Coding & Development

Using AI to Generate and Optimize Code

The Role of AI in Software Development

Artificial intelligence has significantly transformed software development by **assisting in writing, optimizing, debugging, and refactoring code**. AI models like **ChatGPT, Bard, Claude, and Copilot** can generate **structured, functional, and efficient** code across multiple programming languages. However, using AI for coding requires **effective prompts** to ensure accurate, optimized, and secure output.

Why Use AI for Code Generation?

Increases productivity – AI generates code snippets **quickly**, reducing manual effort.
Optimizes efficiency – AI can suggest **faster, optimized algorithms** and **memory-efficient** code.
Improves readability – AI can restructure complex code into **clean, readable formats**.
Enhances learning – Developers can use AI as an **interactive coding assistant** to learn best practices.

---

1. Using AI to Generate Code

Best Practices for AI-Generated Code Prompts

- **Specify the programming language** – Avoid generic prompts; define the **required syntax**.
- **Define the functionality** – Provide **clear details on the expected behavior** of the code.

- **Request best practices** – Ask AI to **follow coding standards** like PEP 8 (Python) or SOLID principles.
- **Ensure error handling** – Specify that the AI should include **exception handling** and **input validation**.

---

2. Example Prompts for AI-Generated Code

Basic Function Prompt

"Write a Python function to calculate the factorial of a number using recursion."

Object-Oriented Programming (OOP) Prompt

"Generate a Java class named 'Employee' with attributes for name, ID, and salary. Include getters, setters, and a method to calculate an annual bonus."

Web Development Prompt

"Write an HTML, CSS, and JavaScript code snippet for a responsive login form with basic input validation."

Database Query Prompt

"Generate an SQL query to fetch all customers who made purchases above $500 in the last 30 days."

Machine Learning Model Prompt

"Create a Python script using TensorFlow to build and train a neural network for image classification."

---

3. AI for Code Optimization

AI can **refactor code** to improve **efficiency, readability, and performance** by:
   Reducing redundant logic – AI can simplify loops and conditionals.
   Enhancing performance – AI optimizes algorithms for **time and space complexity**.

Adhering to best practices – AI suggests **cleaner and more structured coding styles**.

Example: Optimizing Code with AI

Prompt:
"Optimize the following Python function to improve efficiency and reduce time complexity:"

python
CopyEdit
```python
def find_duplicates(nums):
    duplicates = []
    for i in range(len(nums)):
        for j in range(i+1, len(nums)):
            if nums[i] == nums[j] and nums[i] not in duplicates:
                duplicates.append(nums[i])
    return duplicates
```

AI-Optimized Output:

python
CopyEdit
```python
def find_duplicates(nums):
    seen, duplicates = set(), set()
    for num in nums:
        if num in seen:
            duplicates.add(num)
        seen.add(num)
    return list(duplicates)
```

Time Complexity Reduced from $O(n^2)$ to $O(n)$ using a **set-based approach**.

Debugging with AI: Strengths and Limitations

1. Strengths of AI in Debugging

AI is particularly useful for debugging because it can:
  Identify syntax errors – AI detects missing parentheses, colons, and incorrect syntax.
  Suggest logical fixes – AI explains errors and provides **suggested corrections**.
  Automate unit testing – AI can generate **test cases** to validate code functionality.
  Analyze performance issues – AI can detect **inefficient loops, memory leaks, and redundant logic**.

2. Example Prompts for AI Debugging Assistance

Identifying Bugs in a Function

Prompt:
  "I am getting an 'IndexError: list index out of range' in the following Python function. Can you debug and fix it?"

python
CopyEdit
```python
def get_element(lst, index):
    return lst[index]

print(get_element([1, 2, 3], 5))
```

AI Output:

python
CopyEdit
```python
def get_element(lst, index):
    return lst[index] if 0 <= index < len(lst) else "Index out of range"

print(get_element([1, 2, 3], 5))
```

  AI introduces boundary checking to prevent errors.

Fixing a Compilation Error

Prompt:

"My Java code won't compile due to a 'NullPointerException'. Can you identify the issue?"

java
CopyEdit
```java
public class Main {
    public static void main(String[] args) {
        String name;
        System.out.println(name.length());
    }
}
```

AI Output:

java
CopyEdit
```java
public class Main {
    public static void main(String[] args) {
        String name = "Hello"; // Initialize variable to prevent NullPointerException
        System.out.println(name.length());
    }
}
```

AI **fixes uninitialized variables**, ensuring safe execution.

3. Limitations of AI Debugging

While AI is powerful for debugging, it has limitations:

  Lacks Deep Context Awareness – AI may suggest fixes without understanding broader project dependencies.

  Cannot Debug Runtime Issues in Live Applications – AI cannot interact with real-time debugging tools like GDB, Jupyter, or IDE debuggers.

  May Generate Over-Simplified Fixes – AI might suggest fixes that remove errors but introduce logic flaws.

  Does Not Always Consider Security – AI may overlook security vulnerabilities in suggested fixes.

4. Best Practices for Debugging with AI

Best Practice	Description	Example Prompt
Provide Full Error Messages	AI performs better when given **detailed error logs**.	"Fix this Python function that raises a 'TypeError: unsupported operand'."
Explain Expected Behavior	AI works best when it understands **the intended output**.	"My function should return an ordered list, but it's returning duplicates."
Verify AI Fixes	Always **test AI suggestions** to ensure correctness.	"Explain why this AI-generated fix works before I implement it."
Ask for Multiple Solutions	AI may suggest **one approach**, but others might be better.	"Can you suggest three ways to fix this infinite loop issue?"
Ensure AI Includes Best Practices	AI should follow **secure and optimized coding standards**.	"Refactor this function using best practices for performance."

Key Takeaways for AI in Coding & Debugging

AI can generate structured, well-optimized code across multiple languages.
Effective prompts define language, functionality, and best practices for accurate code generation.
AI is a powerful debugging tool but should be used alongside human verification.
AI cannot fully replace real-time debugging tools, but it improves efficiency.
Developers should combine AI assistance with manual testing, security checks, and best coding practices.

By leveraging **AI for code generation, optimization, and debugging**, developers can **enhance productivity and build more efficient, secure applications**. However, human oversight remains **essential** to ensure **logical correctness, security, and maintainability** in software development.

AI-Assisted Software Documentation and Code Explanations

The Importance of AI in Software Documentation

Software documentation plays a **critical role** in software development, providing essential information about **code functionality, API usage, system architecture, and troubleshooting procedures**. AI can assist developers in **automating and optimizing documentation processes**, ensuring that code is well-explained, readable, and maintainable.

How AI Can Improve Software Documentation

 Generates clear and structured documentation – AI can **automatically document functions, classes, and APIs**.
 Enhances readability for new developers – AI-generated explanations help **onboard new team members faster**.
 Provides real-time documentation updates – AI can **adapt documentation when code changes**.
 Automates inline commenting – AI can add **helpful comments directly into source code**.
 Improves API documentation – AI assists in **generating OpenAPI specifications and SDK guides**.

1. Using AI to Generate Software Documentation

Best Practices for AI-Generated Documentation

- **Specify the programming language** – AI-generated documentation should align with **language-specific conventions**.
- **Request detailed function/class explanations** AI should **explain inputs, outputs, and use cases**.
- **Ensure clarity for different audiences** – Documentation should be readable for **beginners and advanced developers**.
- **Include usage examples** – AI should generate **sample code snippets** to demonstrate functionality.

2. Example Prompts for AI-Generated Documentation

Function Documentation Prompt

"Document the following Python function, including input parameters, return values, and an example of usage:"

python
CopyEdit
```python
def calculate_area(length, width):
    return length * width
```

AI-Generated Documentation:

python
CopyEdit
```python
def calculate_area(length: float, width: float) -> float:
    """
    Calculates the area of a rectangle.

    Parameters:
        length (float): The length of the rectangle.
        width (float): The width of the rectangle.

    Returns:
        float: The computed area of the rectangle.

    Example:
        >>> calculate_area(5, 3)
        15
```

```
    """
    return length * width
```

AI adds a detailed docstring, making the function self-explanatory.

Class Documentation Prompt

"Generate documentation for the following Java class, including method descriptions:"

java
CopyEdit
```java
public class Car {
    private String model;
    private int speed;

    public Car(String model) {
        this.model = model;
        this.speed = 0;
    }

    public void accelerate(int increase) {
        this.speed += increase;
    }

    public int getSpeed() {
        return speed;
    }
}
```

AI-Generated Documentation:

java
CopyEdit
```java
/**
 * Represents a Car with model and speed attributes.
 */
public class Car {
```
115

```java
    private String model;
    private int speed;

    /**
     * Constructs a new Car instance with a specified model.
     *
     * @param model The model name of the car.
     */
    public Car(String model) {
        this.model = model;
        this.speed = 0;
    }

    /**
     * Accelerates the car by a given speed increment.
     *
     * @param increase The amount to increase the speed.
     */
    public void accelerate(int increase) {
        this.speed += increase;
    }

    /**
     * Retrieves the current speed of the car.
     *
     * @return The current speed of the car.
     */
    public int getSpeed() {
        return speed;
    }
}
```

AI generates structured JavaDocs, improving maintainability.

3. AI-Assisted Code Explanation

AI can **analyze existing code and explain it in simpler terms**, helping developers understand complex logic quickly.

Code Explanation Prompt Example

"Explain the purpose and functionality of this Python script in simple terms:"

python
CopyEdit
```python
def is_palindrome(s):
    s = s.lower().replace(" ", "")
    return s == s[::-1]

print(is_palindrome("Racecar"))
```

AI-Generated Explanation:
 "This function checks if a given string is a palindrome. It first converts the string to lowercase and removes spaces to ensure uniformity. Then, it compares the string with its reverse (`s[::-1]`). If both match, the function returns `True`, indicating that the input is a palindrome."
 AI provides a beginner-friendly explanation.

Refactoring Suggestions Prompt

"Suggest improvements to the following JavaScript function for better readability and efficiency:"

javascript
CopyEdit
```javascript
function reverseString(str) {
    let reversed = "";
    for (let i = str.length - 1; i >= 0; i--) {
        reversed += str[i];
    }
    return reversed;
}
```

117

AI-Generated Refactored Code:

```javascript
javascript
CopyEdit
function reverseString(str) {
    return str.split("").reverse().join("");
}
```

AI optimizes the function using built-in JavaScript methods.

Table: Examples of Effective Coding Prompts

Prompt Type	Example Prompt	AI Output Expectation
Code Generation	"Generate a Python script to sort a list of numbers using quicksort."	A complete **Python quicksort implementation**.
Function Documentation	"Document this C++ function with proper comments."	AI provides a **docstring with function details, parameters, and return values**.
Code Explanation	"Explain how this Java recursion function works."	AI **breaks down the recursive logic** in simple terms.
Code Optimization	"Improve this SQL query for faster execution."	AI suggests **indexing, joins, or query restructuring**.
Bug Fixing	"Fix this JavaScript function throwing an	AI **identifies and corrects the missing variable definition**.

	undefined variable error."	
API Documentation	"Write API documentation for this Express.js route."	AI **creates a structured API doc with request/response details**.
Code Refactoring	"Simplify this Java loop without changing its logic."	AI **converts loops to cleaner, optimized formats**.

Key Takeaways for AI-Assisted Documentation & Code Explanations

AI improves software documentation by automating function, class, and API descriptions.

Code explanation prompts help developers quickly understand complex scripts.

AI can generate structured comments and documentation that follow industry standards.

Well-defined prompts ensure AI provides clear, structured, and maintainable documentation.

AI-assisted refactoring and optimization enhance code readability and performance.

By leveraging AI for **code documentation and explanation**, developers can **save time, improve clarity, and maintain high-quality software** with minimal effort.

Chapter 12

AI Prompting for Data Analysis & Research

Generating Reports, Insights, and Visual Data Summaries

The Role of AI in Data Analysis and Research

AI has revolutionized **data analysis, research, and reporting** by automating complex calculations, identifying patterns, and presenting **insightful summaries with visualizations**. AI-powered tools such as **ChatGPT, Bard, Claude, and Python-based libraries (Pandas, Matplotlib, Seaborn, and Scikit-learn)** assist researchers, business analysts, and data scientists in **efficiently processing, interpreting, and visualizing large datasets**.

By structuring prompts effectively, users can leverage AI to **generate in-depth reports, summarize complex datasets, and produce visual data representations** for business intelligence, financial modeling, and academic research.

1. AI for Generating Reports and Data Insights

Best Practices for AI-Powered Report Generation

Define the Report Type – Clearly specify if the report is for **business, finance, healthcare, market research, or academic purposes**.
 Include Data Context – Provide **raw data, key variables, and expected output format**.
 Specify Formatting Requirements – Indicate whether the AI should generate **a structured report, executive summary, or bullet-point analysis**.
 Request Data Interpretation – Ask AI to **explain patterns, correlations, and trends** from the dataset.
 Ensure Data Accuracy – Validate AI-generated insights by cross-referencing **real-time or verified sources**.

2. Example Prompts for AI-Generated Reports

Financial Report Prompt

"Generate a 500-word financial performance report for ABC Corporation, analyzing revenue growth, expense trends, and profit margins for the past five years. Include key financial ratios and a summary of challenges and opportunities."

Market Research Report Prompt

"Summarize the latest trends in the global electric vehicle market, focusing on market size, key players, consumer preferences, and regulatory influences. Provide insights into future growth projections."

Academic Research Summary Prompt

"Summarize the key findings from this dataset on climate change impact over the last decade. Identify trends, anomalies, and policy implications."

Healthcare Data Insights Prompt

"Analyze the following dataset containing patient demographics, medical history, and disease occurrence rates. Identify correlations between lifestyle factors and disease prevalence. Present findings in a structured report."

3. AI for Visual Data Summaries

The Importance of Data Visualization in Research

Data visualization helps **simplify complex datasets**, making insights more accessible and actionable. AI can generate **charts, graphs, heatmaps, and dashboards** that transform raw data into **meaningful representations**.

Enhances data-driven decision-making
Identifies trends, correlations, and anomalies
Improves report readability for non-technical stakeholders
Reduces cognitive load by replacing large datasets with visual summaries

---

4. Example Prompts for AI-Generated Data Visualizations

Generating a Bar Chart for Sales Performance

121

"Create a bar chart showing the monthly sales performance of an e-commerce company for the past 12 months. Highlight the top three highest revenue months."

Creating a Line Graph for Stock Market Trends

"Generate a line graph illustrating the stock price movement of Tesla (TSLA) over the past five years. Indicate major market events that influenced price fluctuations."

Producing a Heatmap for Customer Preferences

"Generate a heatmap to visualize customer preferences for different product categories based on purchase frequency. Use color gradients to highlight the most and least popular products."

Building a Pie Chart for Market Share Analysis

"Create a pie chart displaying the market share distribution of leading smartphone manufacturers in 2024. Represent the top five brands and include an 'Others' category."

AI for Market Research and Predictive Analysis

The Role of AI in Market Research

AI streamlines market research by **collecting, analyzing, and summarizing** large volumes of **consumer data, competitor strategies, and industry trends**. It assists businesses in **understanding market demand, forecasting sales, and identifying new growth opportunities**.

Tracks real-time market trends and consumer sentiment
Analyzes competitor strategies and pricing models
Forecasts future sales and demand patterns
Identifies potential business expansion opportunities

1. AI-Driven Market Research Insights

Consumer Behavior Analysis Prompt

"Analyze consumer buying patterns in the fashion industry over the past five years. Identify trends, key influencing factors, and predictions for future shopping habits."

Competitive Landscape Report Prompt

"Compare the digital marketing strategies of Nike, Adidas, and Puma. Highlight their strengths, weaknesses, and social media engagement effectiveness."

Sentiment Analysis of Customer Reviews

"Analyze 10,000 customer reviews of Apple's latest iPhone. Identify common themes, sentiment trends (positive, negative, neutral), and areas of improvement."

Global Industry Growth Forecast

"Generate a market forecast report for the renewable energy industry in 2030. Predict growth in solar, wind, and hydro energy adoption based on current investment trends."

2. AI for Predictive Analytics

Predictive analytics uses AI models to **forecast future events** based on historical data. Industries such as **finance, healthcare, retail, and manufacturing** rely on predictive models to **optimize strategies and reduce risks**.

Forecasts customer demand and sales revenue
Predicts financial market trends and stock performance
Identifies high-risk patients in healthcare for preventive treatment
Optimizes supply chain management to reduce disruptions

3. Example Prompts for AI-Driven Predictive Analysis

Sales Forecasting Prompt

"Predict the sales performance of a retail company for the next quarter based on historical sales data, seasonality, and current market trends."

Stock Market Trend Prediction Prompt

"Analyze stock price movements of Microsoft (MSFT) over the past five years and predict its price trend for the next 12 months based on economic indicators and historical patterns."

Customer Churn Prediction Prompt

"Identify key risk factors for customer churn in a subscription-based business. Analyze past customer behavior and predict potential churn rates for the next quarter."

Healthcare Risk Prediction Prompt

"Analyze a dataset of patient medical records and predict which patients are at high risk of developing cardiovascular diseases in the next five years. Consider factors like age, lifestyle, and genetic history."

Table: Best Practices for AI-Driven Data Analysis & Research

Best Practice	Description	Example Prompt
Define the Research Scope	Clearly state the focus area of analysis.	"Analyze the impact of inflation on consumer spending in 2024."
Request Data Summarizatio n	Ask AI to provide key takeaways from datasets.	"Summarize the main findings of this financial report in 300 words."
Specify Output Format	Indicate whether results should be in text, tables, or charts.	"Generate a pie chart for market share distribution."
Ensure Data Accuracy	Cross-verify AI-generated insights with real-time data.	"Provide the latest trends in e-commerce with supporting statistics."
Use AI for Predictive Analysis	Forecast future trends based on historical patterns.	"Predict demand for electric vehicles in 2025."
Incorporate Visualizations	Request AI-generated graphs for better clarity.	"Create a bar chart of revenue growth over five years."

Key Takeaways for AI in Data Analysis & Research

AI can automate report generation, data interpretation, and trend analysis.
Well-structured prompts ensure accurate, insightful, and actionable research.
AI-generated visualizations enhance data presentation and simplify complex datasets.
Predictive analytics help businesses forecast future trends and optimize decision-making.
AI should always be used alongside human validation to ensure accuracy and reliability.

By effectively leveraging **AI for data-driven insights, market research, and predictive modeling**, businesses and researchers can **make informed, strategic decisions with confidence**.

How to Structure Data-Driven Prompts for AI

The Importance of Well-Structured Prompts in Data Analysis

AI models are powerful tools for **processing, analyzing, and interpreting data**, but their effectiveness depends heavily on how prompts are structured. A **well-designed prompt** provides AI with **clear instructions, context, and output expectations**, ensuring the generated insights are **relevant, accurate, and actionable**.

1. Key Components of a Well-Structured Data-Driven Prompt

A structured AI prompt for data analysis should include the following elements:

Component	Purpose	Example

125

Objective	Define the purpose of the analysis.	"Analyze sales trends over the past five years."
Data Context	Provide relevant dataset details or key variables.	"Dataset includes monthly revenue, customer demographics, and product categories."
Specific Task	Clearly state what insights are needed.	"Identify top-performing product categories by revenue contribution."
Preferred Output Format	Specify whether the output should be a **summary, table, visualization, or model.**	"Generate a bar chart ranking product sales by category."
Constraints & Filters	Define **date ranges, specific variables, or conditions.**	"Focus only on data from 2020 to 2024 for North America."
Actionability	Indicate how the insights will be used.	"Provide recommendations based on sales trends."

2. Example Prompts for AI-Powered Data Analysis

Sales Performance Analysis

"Analyze sales data from 2019 to 2024 and identify revenue trends, seasonal variations, and high-performing product categories. Present the findings in a structured table and provide a brief summary of key insights."

Customer Segmentation for Marketing

"Using customer purchase history, segment the customer base into high-value, mid-value, and low-value groups. Identify their buying patterns and suggest targeted marketing strategies for each segment."

Financial Report Generation

"Generate a quarterly financial performance summary for ABC Corporation, highlighting revenue growth, profit margins, and cost variations. Include key financial ratios and a comparative analysis of the past four quarters."

Market Trend Prediction

"Predict demand for electric vehicles in 2025 based on historical sales data, government policies, and emerging consumer preferences. Present the prediction in a line graph with key influencing factors highlighted."

Healthcare Risk Assessment

"Analyze a dataset of patient medical records and predict the probability of developing cardiovascular diseases within five years. Use risk factors such as age, BMI, smoking history, and cholesterol levels. Summarize findings in a risk assessment table."

Stock Market Insights

"Examine stock price movements of Tesla (TSLA) over the past five years. Identify trends, major influencing factors, and project the expected price range for the next 12 months based on historical patterns."

---

3. Illustration: AI-Powered Data Analysis Flowchart

The flowchart below visually represents how AI processes **structured data-driven prompts** to generate insightful outputs:

plaintext
CopyEdit

```
+-------------------------------------------------------+
                  |   User Provides Structured Data Prompt
  |
                  |   (Defines Objective, Variables, Output
Type)   |
```

```
+----------------------------------------------------+
                                          |
                                          v

+----------------------------------------------------+
                    |   AI Interprets Data Context &
Requirements     |

+----------------------------------------------------+
                                          |
                                          v

+----------------------------------------------------+
                    |   AI Fetches and Analyzes Data
  |
                    |   - Identifies trends & patterns
  |
                    |   - Applies statistical or ML models
  |
                    |   - Summarizes key insights
  |

+----------------------------------------------------+
                                          |
                                          v
                    |  Does the output meet user-defined
criteria?    |
                         (Yes)                      |           (No)
                           |                        |
                           v                        v
          +------------------------------+
+---------------------------------+
          | AI Generates Report, Graphs,  | | AI Refines Analysis
& Adjusts  |
          | or Predictive Model Output    | | Based on User
Feedback          |
```
128

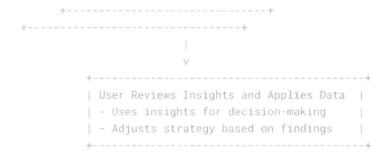

```
        +--------------------------------+
     +--------------------------------+  |
     |                                |  |
                      |
                      V
     +------------------------------------------+
     | User Reviews Insights and Applies Data   |
     | - Uses insights for decision-making      |
     | - Adjusts strategy based on findings     |
     +------------------------------------------+
```

4. Best Practices for Structuring AI Data Prompts

Best Practice	Description	Example Prompt
Be Specific & Clear	Define exactly what insights are needed.	"Analyze customer retention rates over the past 3 years."
Request Structured Outputs	Ask for tables, charts, or summaries.	"Provide findings in a summary table with key metrics."
Filter Data for Relevance	Narrow down results using specific conditions.	"Focus only on transactions above $500 in 2023."
Use Contextual Prompts	Provide dataset details or expected patterns.	"Compare revenue growth before and after marketing campaigns."
Refine and Iterate	Adjust prompts based on initial AI responses.	"Expand analysis to include customer demographics."

Key Takeaways for Structuring AI-Powered Data Analysis Prompts

129

A well-structured prompt improves AI accuracy and relevance in data analysis.

Defining objectives, filters, and expected outputs ensures precise insights.

AI-generated visualizations enhance the clarity of complex data findings.

Iterative refinement of prompts improves the quality of AI-generated reports.

Using AI for market research, finance, healthcare, and predictive analysis accelerates data-driven decision-making.

By following these structured approaches, businesses, researchers, and analysts can maximize **AI's capabilities in data interpretation, trend analysis, and predictive modeling**, leading to **faster, data-backed decision-making**.

Chapter 13

AI Prompting for Business & Marketing

AI in Digital Marketing, Sales Copy, and Customer Engagement

The Role of AI in Modern Business and Marketing

Artificial Intelligence (AI) has transformed the way businesses operate, especially in **digital marketing, sales copywriting, and customer engagement**. Companies use AI to automate content creation, personalize marketing strategies, optimize sales funnels, and enhance customer interaction.

AI-powered tools like **ChatGPT, Bard, Claude, and Copy.ai** assist marketers in:
Generating persuasive sales copy that drives conversions.
Personalizing marketing campaigns based on customer preferences.
Automating customer interactions through AI chatbots and virtual assistants.
Improving lead nurturing strategies with AI-driven insights.
Optimizing content for search engines (SEO) and improving click-through rates (CTR).

---

1. AI in Digital Marketing

How AI Enhances Digital Marketing Strategies

Personalization at Scale – AI customizes content and promotions for different audience segments.
Data-Driven Decision Making – AI analyzes customer behavior and recommends optimized marketing strategies.
SEO and Content Optimization – AI tools help structure content for higher search rankings.
Social Media Automation – AI schedules, optimizes, and personalizes posts for

maximum engagement.

A/B Testing at Speed – AI runs multiple ad variations simultaneously to determine the best-performing copy.

Example AI-Powered Digital Marketing Prompts

SEO-Optimized Blog Post Prompt

"Generate a 1,500-word SEO-friendly article on 'Top E-commerce Trends in 2025.' Use keywords like 'e-commerce growth,' 'AI in shopping,' and 'future retail technologies.' Include a compelling introduction and actionable takeaways."

Social Media Ad Copy Prompt

"Write a high-converting Facebook ad for a new organic skincare brand. Emphasize natural ingredients, sustainability, and a limited-time discount. Include a compelling call-to-action."

Instagram Caption Prompt

"Create an engaging Instagram caption for a fitness apparel brand launching a new line of moisture-wicking gym wear. Keep it motivational, include two trending fitness hashtags, and encourage engagement with a question."

Google Ads Copy Prompt

"Write three variations of a Google Ad for a digital marketing agency offering SEO services. Focus on lead generation, high ROI, and expert strategies."

---

2. AI for Sales Copywriting

How AI Helps Write Persuasive Sales Copy

Creates compelling headlines and taglines for advertisements.
A/B tests different variations of ad copy to determine the best performer.
Crafts persuasive product descriptions that highlight features and benefits.
Writes landing page copy designed to increase conversions.
Improves call-to-action (CTA) effectiveness to drive immediate responses.

Example AI-Powered Sales Copywriting Prompts

Landing Page Copy Prompt

"Write a high-converting landing page copy for an AI-powered writing assistant. Emphasize ease of use, time-saving benefits, and pricing plans. Include a CTA for a free trial."

E-commerce Product Description Prompt

"Generate an engaging product description for a wireless noise-canceling headphone. Highlight key features like battery life, comfort, and immersive sound experience."

Persuasive CTA Prompt

"Create a compelling call-to-action for an online course on AI marketing. Make it urgent and persuasive to encourage sign-ups."

3. AI for Customer Engagement

How AI Enhances Customer Interactions

Chatbots and Virtual Assistants – AI-driven chatbots provide instant responses and improve customer satisfaction.
Personalized Email Campaigns – AI tailors email content based on customer behavior.
Predictive Analytics for Customer Retention – AI anticipates customer needs and prevents churn.
Automated Follow-Ups – AI nurtures leads with strategic follow-up sequences.
Voice Assistants for Customer Service – AI enhances customer interactions through voice-based solutions.

Example AI-Powered Customer Engagement Prompts

AI Chatbot Script Prompt

"Write a chatbot script for an e-commerce store that assists customers with product recommendations, shipping inquiries, and order tracking."

Customer Service Email Response Prompt

"Write a professional yet empathetic response to a customer complaint about a delayed shipment. Offer a discount coupon as compensation."

AI-Generated Customer Follow-Up Prompt

"Create a follow-up email sequence for a potential customer who added a product to their cart but didn't complete the purchase."

Creating Highly Converting Email Sequences with AI

Why AI-Generated Email Sequences Are Effective

Saves Time – AI can draft entire email campaigns within minutes.
Increases Personalization – AI customizes emails based on customer behavior and preferences.
Improves Open and Click-Through Rates – AI optimizes subject lines and CTAs for better engagement.
A/B Testing Optimization – AI tests multiple variations of emails to find the best-performing version.

---

1. Structuring an AI-Generated Email Sequence

A well-designed email sequence typically includes:

Email Type	Purpose	Example Subject Line
Welcome Email	Introduce the brand and set expectations.	"Welcome! Here's What to Expect from Us "
Lead Nurturing Email	Educate the customer about the product/service.	"How Our AI Assistant Can Save You Hours Every Day"

Promotional Email	Highlight special offers and incentives.	"Limited-Time Offer: 20% Off Our AI Writing Tool!"
Cart Abandonmen t Email	Recover lost sales from unfinished checkouts.	"Forget Something? Complete Your Purchase Today!"
Customer Retention Email	Keep customers engaged post-purchase.	"Your Next Step: Exclusive Offers Just for You"

2. Example AI-Powered Email Sequences

Welcome Email Prompt

"Write a warm and engaging welcome email for a new subscriber to a fitness coaching program. Highlight key program benefits and encourage engagement with a free resource."

Lead Nurturing Email Prompt

"Create an email educating potential customers about the benefits of AI-powered content generation. Address common concerns and showcase case studies."

Limited-Time Offer Email Prompt

"Write a high-converting promotional email offering 30% off an AI-based grammar checking tool for a limited time. Create urgency and include a persuasive CTA."

Cart Abandonment Email Prompt

"Write a follow-up email reminding a customer that they left items in their cart. Offer a 10% discount if they complete the purchase within 24 hours."

Post-Purchase Thank You Email Prompt

"Write a thank-you email for a customer who purchased a digital marketing course. Include bonus resources and encourage them to share feedback."

135

Key Takeaways for AI in Business & Marketing

 AI improves marketing efficiency by automating content creation, personalization, and optimization.
 AI-driven sales copywriting enhances persuasiveness, engagement, and conversions.
 AI-powered email sequences increase customer retention and revenue growth.
 Using structured prompts ensures AI-generated marketing materials align with business goals.
 AI chatbots and automation tools improve customer support and lead nurturing.

By leveraging **AI for marketing, sales, and customer engagement**, businesses can **increase efficiency, drive higher conversions, and create more personalized customer experiences**—ultimately leading to higher **revenue growth and brand success**.

Writing AI-Generated Product Descriptions and Ads

The Role of AI in Product Descriptions and Advertising

AI is revolutionizing **e-commerce, advertising, and digital marketing** by automating **high-quality, persuasive product descriptions and ad copy**. AI-powered tools like **ChatGPT, Bard, Claude, and Copy.ai** generate **engaging, keyword-optimized, and conversion-driven** marketing content in seconds.

Why Use AI for Product Descriptions and Ads?

Increases Efficiency – AI writes hundreds of descriptions in **minutes**.
 Optimizes SEO – AI integrates relevant **keywords** for higher search rankings.
 Improves Conversion Rates – AI tailors descriptions for **persuasion and emotional appeal**.
 A/B Testing Variations – AI generates multiple versions for **performance testing**.
136

Enhances Brand Consistency – AI ensures **uniform tone and messaging** across product listings.

---

1. AI-Generated Product Descriptions

Best Practices for AI-Generated Product Descriptions

Highlight Features & Benefits – Clearly state what the product does and why it's valuable.

Use Persuasive Language – Focus on **storytelling and emotional triggers** to engage buyers.

Optimize for SEO – Include **keywords** that improve discoverability on search engines and e-commerce platforms.

Format for Readability – Use **bullet points, bold text, and structured paragraphs** for easy scanning.

Incorporate a Call-to-Action (CTA) – Encourage customers to **make a purchase** or **learn more**.

---

2. Example Prompts for AI-Generated Product Descriptions

Electronics Product Description Prompt

"Write a compelling product description for a 4K Smart TV. Highlight key features like Ultra HD resolution, Dolby Atmos sound, and built-in streaming apps. Use persuasive and engaging language."

AI-Generated Output:

Experience Entertainment Like Never Before

Upgrade your home theater with the **4K Ultra HD Smart TV**. Enjoy **stunning picture clarity**, **vibrant colors**, and **Dolby Atmos immersive sound**. With built-in **Netflix, Hulu, and Disney+**, your favorite shows are just a click away. Plus, **voice control and AI-powered recommendations** make it easier than ever to find content you love.

Available now with free shipping. Order today!

Beauty Product Description Prompt

"Generate a luxury-inspired product description for an anti-aging serum. Emphasize hydration, skin rejuvenation, and dermatologist-approved formula."

AI-Generated Output:
Reveal Radiant, Youthful Skin
Indulge in the power of science and luxury with our **Advanced Anti-Aging Serum**. Formulated with **hyaluronic acid, vitamin C, and retinol**, this serum **hydrates, firms, and restores elasticity** for a youthful glow. Clinically tested and **dermatologist-approved**, it visibly reduces fine lines and dark spots.

Transform your skincare routine today!

Fashion Product Description Prompt

"Create a trendy and engaging product description for a new line of sustainable athletic wear."

AI-Generated Output:
Style Meets Sustainability
Move with confidence in our **EcoFlex Athletic Wear**, designed for those who demand both **performance and sustainability**. Made from **100% recycled fabric**, this breathable, moisture-wicking apparel keeps you comfortable from **yoga sessions to high-intensity workouts**.

Eco-friendly. Stylish. Performance-driven. Get yours now!

---

3. AI-Generated Ad Copy

How AI Enhances Ad Copywriting

Generates multiple ad variations for A/B testing.
Incorporates high-converting CTA phrases.
Optimizes word choice for emotional impact.
Personalizes ads for different audience segments.

---

4. Example Prompts for AI-Generated Ad Copy

Facebook Ad Prompt

"Write a high-converting Facebook ad for a fitness tracker, focusing on health benefits, smart technology, and an exclusive discount."

AI-Generated Output:
Get Fitter. Stay Smarter.
Track your fitness goals effortlessly with the **XtremeFit Smart Tracker**.
24/7 Heart Rate Monitoring
Sleep & Activity Tracking
Custom Workout Insights

Limited Offer: 20% OFF Today! Click below to grab yours.

Shop Now!

Instagram Ad Prompt

"Create an Instagram ad for a luxury perfume brand. Use an aspirational and sensory-driven tone."

AI-Generated Output:
Indulge in Elegance. Captivate the Senses.
Introducing **Euphoria Noir**, the fragrance of sophistication. With **rich floral notes, warm vanilla, and a hint of mystery**, this scent is designed to leave a lasting impression.

Discover luxury. Order today.

Google Ad Prompt

"Generate three variations of a Google Ad for an online coding bootcamp. Focus on career advancement, affordability, and flexible learning."

AI-Generated Output:
1 **Become a Software Engineer in 12 Weeks!**
Fast-track your tech career with our **online coding bootcamp**. No experience required.

Enroll Today & Start Learning!

2 **Learn to Code & Get Hired**
Join our **career-focused bootcamp** and land your **dream job in tech**. Flexible, affordable, job-ready skills.

Apply Now!

3 **Master Coding. Change Your Future.**
Learn **Python, JavaScript, and AI development** from industry experts. 100% online. **Pay later options available!**

Start Learning Today!

Table: AI Marketing Prompts and Expected Outcomes

Prompt Type	Example Prompt	Expected AI-Generated Outcome
Product Description	"Write a persuasive description for wireless earbuds with noise cancellation."	A detailed, engaging product overview emphasizing key features.
E-commerc e SEO Copy	"Generate an SEO-friendly description for a smart home security system."	Keyword-optimized content with high-ranking search terms.
Facebook Ad	"Create a Facebook ad for a weight loss supplement with a special discount."	A persuasive, conversion-driven ad copy.
Instagram Caption	"Write an Instagram caption for a summer beachwear collection launch."	A catchy, engaging caption with hashtags.

Google Ads	"Generate three variations of a Google Ad for an online learning platform."	Three concise, persuasive ad versions for A/B testing.
Call-to-Acti on (CTA)	"Write a compelling CTA for an exclusive software deal."	Strong, action-driven messaging to increase conversions.
Promotiona l Email Subject	"Write an attention-grabbing subject line for a 48-hour flash sale."	High-impact email subject to improve open rates.
Landing Page Headline	"Craft a compelling landing page headline for a freelance job marketplace."	A powerful first impression that drives sign-ups.

Key Takeaways for AI in Product Descriptions & Ads

 AI speeds up product listing creation while maintaining quality and persuasion.
 Structured prompts ensure descriptions are engaging, SEO-friendly, and high-converting.
 AI-generated ad copy increases click-through rates and customer engagement.
 A/B testing multiple AI-generated variations optimizes marketing performance.
 Combining AI creativity with human editing results in superior marketing content.

By leveraging **AI for product descriptions and advertising**, businesses can **scale content creation, enhance ad performance, and drive more sales—all while saving time and resources.**

Chapter 14

Bias, Ethics, and Responsible AI Prompting

Recognizing Bias in AI Responses

Understanding AI Bias

AI models generate responses based on the data they are trained on. If that data contains imbalances, stereotypes, or limited perspectives, AI responses can reflect bias, misinformation, or unintentional discrimination. Bias in AI can manifest in various ways, including:

- **Historical Bias:** AI reflects outdated societal norms present in its training data.
- **Cultural Bias:** AI overrepresents dominant cultures and underrepresents marginalized groups.
- **Confirmation Bias:** AI reinforces commonly repeated opinions instead of presenting diverse viewpoints.
- **Gender and Racial Bias:** AI may reproduce stereotypes in content related to gender, ethnicity, or professional roles.
- **Data Bias:** AI favors the perspectives found in the majority of its training data while neglecting less-documented viewpoints.

By identifying these biases, users can critically evaluate AI-generated content and take steps to mitigate distortions and inaccuracies.

Examples of AI Bias in Responses

Example 1: Gender Bias in Professions

Prompt: *"Describe a successful CEO."*

Biased AI Response: *"A CEO is a confident, driven man who leads his company to success with strategic decision-making and leadership."*

Revised AI Response (Bias-Free): *"A CEO is a confident and strategic leader who drives business success through vision, decision-making, and effective management, regardless of gender."*

Example 2: Cultural Bias in History

Prompt: *"Who contributed the most to scientific advancements?"*

Biased AI Response: *"Most major scientific advancements were made by European and American scientists in the last 200 years."*

Revised AI Response (Bias-Free): *"Scientific advancements have come from diverse cultures across history, including contributions from ancient Egyptian, Chinese, Indian, Islamic, African, and European scholars."*

Recognizing biased outputs allows users to adjust prompts and encourage broader perspectives to reduce AI's reliance on dominant but incomplete narratives.

Ensuring Ethical and Inclusive AI Outputs

Principles of Ethical AI Use

To generate responsible AI outputs, users should follow these key principles:

1. **Neutral and Inclusive Language** – Frame prompts to avoid assumptions, stereotypes, or exclusionary wording.
2. **Diverse Perspectives** – Encourage AI to consider multiple viewpoints in responses.
3. **Fact-Checking and Verification** – Cross-reference AI-generated content with reliable sources.
4. **Avoid Reinforcing Harmful Stereotypes** – Ensure AI does not perpetuate biased or offensive statements.
5. **Transparency and Accountability** – Use AI responsibly and disclose AI-generated content when appropriate.

Techniques for Ethical Prompt Engineering

Strategy	Example Prompt	Ethical Impact
Encourage Multiple Perspectives	"Discuss the role of women in STEM fields from a global perspective."	Reduces gender bias and highlights contributions beyond dominant narratives.
Use Neutral Language	"Describe a leader's qualities" instead of "Describe a great businessman."	Avoids gender bias in professional roles.
Request Inclusive Responses	"Provide a culturally diverse list of historical figures in mathematics."	Ensures representation from various regions and eras.
Fact-Check AI Output	"What is the history of artificial intelligence?"	Helps verify AI-generated claims against authoritative sources.
Mitigate Stereotypes	"Describe different parenting styles across cultures."	Prevents AI from favoring a single cultural norm.

By carefully structuring prompts, users can guide AI toward more ethical and inclusive outputs, preventing reinforcement of stereotypes, discrimination, or misinformation.

Case Study: Bias in AI Image and Text Generation

AI models trained on internet datasets have sometimes reflected societal biases in visual and textual outputs. For instance:

- Facial Recognition Bias – Some AI systems have had higher error rates in identifying people of color due to imbalanced training data.
- Text-Based Stereotypes – AI-generated writing has historically overrepresented men in leadership roles while underrepresenting women and minority groups.

To counteract these issues, organizations and AI developers are actively working on:

- Expanding datasets to include diverse voices, languages, and experiences.
- Regular auditing and updating of AI models to detect and correct bias.
- Transparency reports explaining AI decision-making and data sources.

Users can contribute to ethical AI use by actively identifying, reporting, and refining AI-generated outputs to ensure more fairness and accuracy.

Key Takeaways for Ethical and Responsible AI Prompting

- Bias in AI originates from training data and user prompts. Recognizing and mitigating bias ensures more balanced AI responses.
- Ethical AI prompting requires neutral language, inclusive framing, and multi-perspective responses.
- Fact-checking AI-generated outputs is crucial to prevent misinformation.
- By using well-structured prompts, users can guide AI toward fair, diverse, and responsible content.

With thoughtful prompting techniques, AI can serve as an informative and equitable tool, helping to enhance knowledge, bridge gaps, and promote inclusivity in the digital age.

Strategies for Reducing AI Bias Through Prompting

Understanding AI Bias and Its Impact

AI bias refers to **systematic errors or unfair assumptions** in AI-generated content due to **skewed training data, algorithmic design, or prompt structuring**. Bias in AI can lead to:

Inaccurate or misleading information
 Unfair or discriminatory responses
 Exclusion of diverse perspectives
 Reinforcement of stereotypes

By implementing **strategic prompting techniques**, we can **minimize AI bias** and ensure **fair, inclusive, and objective outputs** across different domains, including **business, marketing, research, and AI-generated content creation**.

---

1. How AI Bias is Formed

AI bias originates from **three main sources**:

Type of Bias	Cause	Example
Data Bias	AI models learn from **historical data**, which may reflect societal biases.	A job-matching AI prioritizing male candidates for leadership roles due to past hiring trends.

Algorithmic Bias	AI may **favor certain patterns** in data due to model design.	An AI chatbot generating **Western-centric** travel recommendations instead of global ones.
Prompting Bias	Unintentionally **leading or vague prompts** can skew responses.	Asking AI, "Why are startups always run by young people?" may reinforce an age bias instead of exploring diverse entrepreneurship.

2. Strategies for Reducing AI Bias Through Prompting

A. Use Neutral, Non-Leading Language

Biased Prompt:
"Why are electric cars better than gasoline cars?"

Bias-Free Prompt:
"Compare the benefits and drawbacks of electric cars and gasoline cars."

By **removing biased wording** like "better," the AI produces a more **balanced analysis**.

B. Request Diverse Perspectives

AI often defaults to the **most commonly available information**. Requesting **diverse viewpoints** ensures **more inclusive outputs**.

Diversity-Oriented Prompts:

- *"Provide multiple perspectives on the impact of remote work on employee productivity."*
- *"Summarize the history of AI development across different countries, including contributions from Asia, Europe, and Africa."*

147

- *"Discuss gender representation in STEM fields with examples from various regions."*

This approach **encourages AI to consider multiple viewpoints** instead of defaulting to **one dominant narrative**.

C. Specify Fact-Checking and Source Attribution

AI sometimes generates **misleading or factually incorrect information** due to training data limitations. Adding **fact-checking constraints** improves accuracy.

Fact-Checking Prompts:

- *"Summarize the latest trends in renewable energy. Ensure responses are based on verified industry reports."*
- *"Provide statistics on global literacy rates, citing the latest available data."*
- *"Give an overview of climate change policies worldwide, referencing regional differences."*

This encourages AI to **base responses on credible sources** rather than generalizations.

D. Avoid Overgeneralization and Request Specifics

Overgeneralized Prompt:
"What do customers want in an e-commerce platform?"

Specific and Contextualized Prompt:
"Identify the top customer preferences in e-commerce platforms based on different demographics, such as age, region, and purchase behavior."

This ensures **AI accounts for variability in preferences** rather than producing **one-size-fits-all responses**.

E. Implement Multi-Turn Prompting for Depth

Rather than relying on a **single prompt**, use **multi-step follow-ups** to refine responses.

Example Multi-Turn Prompting:

1 *"Summarize gender disparities in tech leadership roles."*
2 *"Now, provide examples of initiatives addressing these disparities."*
3 *"Can you compare success rates of these initiatives across different industries?"*

This **prevents AI from generating surface-level or one-dimensional responses**.

F. Reinforce Ethical AI Considerations

Adding **explicit ethical constraints** ensures AI generates **responsible and unbiased** responses.

Ethical Prompting Examples:

- *"Describe the role of AI in hiring. Ensure fairness, inclusion, and bias reduction are considered."*
- *"Analyze the challenges of AI in criminal justice while addressing ethical concerns."*
- *"Provide an unbiased summary of political ideologies without favoring any perspective."*

This approach **actively discourages AI from reinforcing stereotypes or biased viewpoints**.

3. Illustration: How AI Bias is Formed and Mitigated

The following flowchart outlines **how AI bias develops and how effective prompting can counteract it**.

plaintext
CopyEdit

```
+------------------------------------------------------+
           | AI Model Trained on Historical Data

|

+------------------------------------------------------+
```

```
                                   |
                                   v
+------------------------------------------------------------+
        | Potential Bias from Skewed Data or Algorithm Design
|
+------------------------------------------------------------+
                                   |
                                   v
+------------------------------------------------------------+
        | User Inputs Prompt
|
        | (Leading/Biased or Neutral/Inclusive)
|
+------------------------------------------------------------+
                      |                         |
            (Biased Prompt)          (Unbiased Prompt)
                      |                         |
                      v                         v
+--------------------+          +--------------------------+
| AI Generates       |          | AI Produces              |
| Skewed Response    |          | Balanced, Fact-Based Data |
+--------------------+          +--------------------------+
           |                               |
           v                               v
+------------------+          +--------------------------+
| Reinforces Bias  |          | Reduces Bias through     |
| in AI Outputs    |          | Fact-Checking, Diversity|
+------------------+          +--------------------------+
```

---

4. Best Practices for Bias-Free AI Prompting

150

Strategy	Example Prompt	Bias Reduction Outcome
Use Neutral Language	"Compare different economic systems."	Avoids leading AI toward one ideology.
Request Diverse Perspectives	"Provide global examples of successful AI policies."	Ensures multiple viewpoints are considered.
Ask for Source-Based Insights	"Summarize the impact of climate change using scientific reports."	Encourages fact-based responses.
Avoid Generalizations	"Analyze shopping behavior trends for different age groups."	Prevents one-size-fits-all assumptions.
Use Multi-Turn Prompting	"Explain gender disparities in STEM → Suggest solutions → Compare impact across industries."	Improves depth and eliminates surface-level bias.
Explicitly Request Fairness	"Describe AI's impact on hiring with a focus on fairness and ethics."	Encourages unbiased and responsible AI behavior.

Key Takeaways for Reducing AI Bias Through Prompting

AI bias is influenced by data, algorithm design, and user prompts.
Using neutral language and fact-based constraints minimizes bias.
Encouraging diverse perspectives prevents AI from defaulting to dominant narratives.
Multi-turn prompting adds depth and reduces overgeneralization.
Explicit ethical considerations in prompts improve AI fairness.

By adopting **strategic, bias-aware prompting techniques**, users can **enhance AI accuracy, fairness, and inclusivity**, ensuring that AI-generated content remains **reliable, balanced, and ethical**.

Chapter 15

The Future of AI Prompt Engineering

The Evolution of AI Models and Self-Improving Prompts

The Transformation of AI Models Over Time

Artificial intelligence has evolved rapidly from **basic rule-based systems** to **self-learning deep learning models** that generate human-like responses. The field of **AI prompt engineering** has progressed alongside these advancements, moving from **static command-based inputs** to **dynamic, context-aware interactions**.

The evolution of AI models follows a **clear trajectory of increased complexity, adaptability, and efficiency**:

Era	Key Advancements	Impact on Prompting
Rule-Based AI (1950s-1980s)	Programs followed explicit commands with predefined rules.	Simple commands with limited flexibility.
Statistical Machine Learning (1990s-2010s)	AI learned from structured datasets to make predictions.	Prompts needed structured data for optimal results.
Deep Learning & NLP (2010s-Present)	AI models trained on vast amounts of data with neural networks.	AI became **context-aware**, requiring well-structured prompts.
Self-Learning & Adaptive AI (2020s-2030s)	AI models continuously refine responses based on interaction.	**Prompts evolve dynamically**,

		adapting to user needs.

With each generation, AI has become **more intuitive, responsive, and capable of understanding nuanced human language**, reducing the need for highly structured prompts while still requiring **strategic input to maximize performance**.

The Rise of Self-Improving Prompts

AI prompting has traditionally been **static**, where a user provides a query, and the AI responds based on pre-existing data. However, the future lies in **self-improving prompts**, where AI:

Learns from past interactions to refine responses.
Adjusts dynamically based on user preferences.
Generates more precise, relevant, and efficient outputs over time.

Self-improving prompts work through **three key mechanisms**:

1. **Memory-Driven Adaptation** – AI remembers past interactions and **tailors responses based on context**.
2. **User Feedback Loops** – AI adjusts prompt structure based on **real-time corrections and refinements**.
3. **Contextual Awareness** – AI integrates external **real-world data** to improve response accuracy.

Example of Self-Improving Prompting

Traditional Prompting:
"Write a summary of blockchain technology."

- AI provides a **generic overview** of blockchain.

Self-Improving Prompting:
"Based on our last discussion on Ethereum, explain how smart contracts revolutionize finance."

- AI **remembers past interactions** and generates **a tailored, in-depth response**.

By **minimizing repetition and maximizing contextual recall**, AI will become increasingly **adaptive, intuitive, and capable of engaging in long-term, complex discussions**.

AI Model Improvements Impacting Prompt Engineering

Future AI Model Capability	Impact on Prompt Engineering
Greater Context Retention	Prompts will become **more conversational** and require **less repetition**.
Emotion & Sentiment Recognition	AI can detect tone, allowing prompts to **influence emotional style**.
Multimodal AI (Text, Image, Voice, Video)	Prompting will involve **cross-medium commands**, such as "Generate an infographic explaining AI ethics."
AI Self-Optimization	AI models will **auto-correct** poorly structured prompts, making them **more efficient**.
Real-Time Learning	AI will dynamically **adjust responses** based on **new information from live sources**.

These advancements will **reduce the burden on users to craft perfect prompts**, as AI will proactively **refine its understanding based on contextual cues**.

Next-Generation AI Assistants and Personalized AI Agents

The Shift Toward Personalized AI Agents

The future of AI lies in **hyper-personalized assistants**, where AI no longer serves as a **generic tool** but rather as a **tailored, adaptive agent** designed to cater to individual users. These **personalized AI assistants** will:

Remember past interactions and user preferences.
Learn user habits, workflows, and communication styles.
Provide proactive recommendations instead of waiting for commands.
Integrate seamlessly across devices, platforms, and applications.

Personal AI agents will shift from **reactive AI** (responding to specific prompts) to **proactive AI** (anticipating user needs before they even ask).

---

1. How Next-Generation AI Assistants Will Work

Feature	Impact on Users
Memory & Personalizatio n	AI will remember preferences, making prompts more fluid and user-specific.
Voice & Gesture Recognition	Users will interact via **speech, gestures, and contextual cues**, not just text.
Automated Task Execution	AI will handle workflows **without manual input** (e.g., "Schedule my meetings and summarize the top three agenda points").
Proactive Assistance	AI will anticipate **emails to respond to, reports to**

	generate, or news to highlight.
Emotionally Intelligent AI	AI will **adjust its tone and recommendations** based on the user's mood or behavior.

AI assistants will evolve into **trusted digital partners**, capable of handling **everything from business strategy to mental health support**.

---

2. Personalized AI Assistants in Different Industries

Industry	AI Assistant Capabilities
Business	AI agents will **draft reports, analyze market trends, and optimize workflows** autonomously.
Healthcare	Personalized AI will **track medical history, suggest treatments, and provide mental health support**.
Education	AI tutors will **adapt lessons based on a student's progress and learning style**.
Marketing	AI will **auto-generate personalized ad campaigns and track performance metrics**.
Finance	AI will **offer investment advice and monitor financial goals** in real-time.

These advancements will create **a seamless AI-powered experience**, where users will rely on AI as **an extension of their decision-making processes**.

---

3. The Future of AI-Human Collaboration

As AI assistants become **more sophisticated**, their role will shift from **passive tools to collaborative partners**. Future AI will:

Augment human creativity – AI will help artists, writers, and developers create unique content.

Enhance decision-making – AI will analyze data and provide **real-time strategic insights**.

Strengthen human-AI teamwork – AI agents will collaborate with humans in **business, research, and innovation**.

The focus will shift from **AI replacing human effort** to **AI enhancing human capabilities**, fostering a future of **co-intelligence and partnership**.

Key Takeaways for the Future of AI Prompt Engineering

AI prompting will evolve from static inputs to dynamic, adaptive interactions.
Self-improving prompts will enable AI to refine responses based on context and memory.
Next-generation AI assistants will become deeply personalized, understanding user habits and preferences.
AI will move from being a reactive tool to a proactive, intelligent agent.
The future will see a seamless AI-human collaboration, where AI enhances productivity, creativity, and strategic thinking.

By understanding and leveraging **the next wave of AI advancements**, individuals and businesses can prepare for **a future where AI is not just a tool—but a thinking partner that enhances every aspect of life.**

AI-Generated Creativity and Its Implications

The Rise of AI in Creative Domains

Artificial intelligence has traditionally been used for **data analysis, automation, and optimization**, but its role in **creative fields** is rapidly expanding. AI is now being used to **generate art, compose music, write literature, design graphics, and develop video content**—blurring the lines between **human and machine creativity**.

With advancements in **generative AI models** such as **DALL·E, MidJourney, ChatGPT, and DeepComposer**, AI is no longer just an analytical tool but a **creative partner**.

 AI-assisted content creation is now widely used in advertising, media, gaming, and design.
  Artists and businesses are leveraging AI for brainstorming, idea generation, and prototype development.
 AI-generated works challenge traditional concepts of authorship, originality, and intellectual property.

Key Creative Fields Where AI is Making an Impact

Creative Field	How AI is Used	Examples
Visual Arts & Design	AI generates artwork, digital designs, and 3D models.	DALL·E, Deep Dream, and AI-assisted graphic design.
Writing & Storytelling	AI helps generate scripts, novels, articles, and marketing copy.	ChatGPT for fiction writing, AI-powered journalism.
Music Composition	AI composes music based on specific styles and emotions.	OpenAI's Jukebox, Google's Magenta for AI music.
Filmmaking & Animation	AI assists in scriptwriting, scene creation, and video editing.	AI-generated movie trailers, automated video summarization.

Game Development	AI creates levels, character designs, and dialogue systems.	AI procedural content generation in video games.

1. Implications of AI-Generated Creativity

The growing role of AI in **creative industries** has sparked debates about **ethics, authorship, and originality**. While AI can enhance human creativity, it also raises **critical questions** about ownership, bias, and artistic value.

A. Ownership & Intellectual Property (IP) Rights

Who owns AI-generated content?
Should AI-generated works receive copyright protection?
How can creators ensure originality when AI is trained on existing art?

These issues are already causing legal debates worldwide, with courts and policymakers determining how to handle **AI-assisted intellectual property**.

B. Creativity vs. Automation

While AI can generate **art, music, and literature**, it still **lacks emotional depth, personal experience, and true self-expression**—elements that define **human creativity**. AI is best viewed as a **collaborative tool**, rather than a replacement for human artists.

AI is great for ideation and rapid prototyping, but lacks deep creative intuition.
Human creators provide emotional depth, nuance, and subjective meaning.
AI can enhance creativity but works best when combined with human vision.

C. Ethical and Cultural Considerations

AI models **learn from existing data**, meaning they can **reproduce biases, cultural stereotypes, or controversial elements** in creative work.

Bias in AI-generated content can reinforce stereotypes.
 AI-generated art should reflect diverse perspectives rather than a narrow dataset.
 Responsible AI use requires ethical guardrails to prevent misuse.

Example: Bias in AI-Generated Art

If an AI is trained primarily on **Western art styles**, it may underrepresent **African, Asian, or Indigenous artistic traditions**, creating a **skewed creative output**.

To address this, AI prompting should **encourage diversity and inclusivity**:

"Generate a painting inspired by Indigenous Australian art techniques."
"Compose a piece of music influenced by traditional Indian ragas."

These strategies help AI **expand creative horizons** beyond **mainstream datasets**.

The Role of Human Oversight in AI-Led Decision Making

Why Human Oversight is Essential

AI is becoming increasingly **autonomous in decision-making**, from **financial investments to medical diagnoses and legal analytics**. While AI improves efficiency and accuracy, **it lacks human judgment, ethical reasoning, and contextual awareness**—making oversight **crucial**.

 AI can analyze vast amounts of data but may misinterpret nuances.
 AI follows logic but cannot always grasp ethical or moral dilemmas.
 AI is trained on past data, which may not account for evolving social, political, or economic changes.

---

1. AI Decision-Making in Critical Fields

Field	How AI is Used	Why Human Oversight is Needed

Healthcare	AI assists in medical diagnosis and treatment planning.	AI can misinterpret rare diseases or misdiagnose based on incomplete data.
Finance	AI predicts stock trends, fraud detection, and risk assessment.	Market crashes and economic instability require human intervention.
Law & Judiciary	AI analyzes legal cases, predicts rulings, and automates contracts.	Legal and ethical judgments involve **morality beyond AI logic**.
Recruitme nt & HR	AI screens job applications based on data patterns.	AI may unintentionally **reinforce biases** present in past hiring data.
Autonomo us Vehicles	AI-powered self-driving technology.	AI cannot always predict **unexpected human behavior or ethical dilemmas**.

2. The Limits of AI in Ethical Decision Making

While AI models can **process patterns and probabilities**, they struggle with **complex moral choices**.

Example: AI in Autonomous Vehicles

If an autonomous car must **choose between swerving into pedestrians or crashing into a barrier**, how should it decide?

AI can **analyze survival probabilities**, but lacks ethical reasoning.
Human oversight is required to **set moral frameworks** for AI-driven decisions.

3. Best Practices for AI-Human Collaboration

AI should **assist decision-making, not replace it**. The best approach is a **hybrid model** where AI and humans work together.

Strategy	Implementation	Impact
Human-in-the-Loop AI	AI makes recommendations, but humans make final decisions.	Ensures ethical oversight and prevents automation risks.
AI Auditing & Regulation	Continuous evaluation of AI decision-making.	Reduces bias, improves accountability.
Transparency in AI Models	Clear explanations of how AI reaches conclusions.	Builds public trust in AI-driven decisions.
Ethical AI Guidelines	Governments and organizations create ethical frameworks.	Ensures AI aligns with societal values.

Key Takeaways for AI-Generated Creativity & Human Oversight

 AI is transforming creative industries but still requires human emotional depth and originality.
 The rise of AI-generated content raises ethical, ownership, and bias concerns.
 AI should be a creative partner, not a replacement for human imagination.
 AI decision-making in critical fields requires human oversight to ensure fairness, ethics, and adaptability.
 The future of AI will depend on responsible governance, human collaboration, and continuous improvements in AI transparency.

By embracing AI **as an augmentation rather than a replacement**, we can **leverage its efficiency while preserving human ingenuity, ethical responsibility, and creative depth.**

www.ingramcontent.com/pod-product-compliance
Lightning Source LLC
LaVergne TN
LVHW022346060326
832902LV00022B/4285